Dancing in

Spirit and

Truth

Lisa

Its wonderful to meet such
beautiful woman of God.
As the Lord leads you
I pray you are blessed
on this journey of life.
I pray you are inspired
and encouraged as you
read.

Blessings and Love
Alicia Pwen

Dancing in Spirit and Truth

Alicia Rivera

Basar Publishing

~Dedication~

To my Lord and Savior Jesus Christ, I dedicate my life and all my works. Thank you Jesus for your great sacrifice. Thank you for my life. Thank you for Grace and Mercy each day.

To my mother Susette Rosado who has always supported, loved, encouraged and inspired me. Mom, I'm thankful that God gave me a wonderful, dedicated mother. You are truly a beautiful righteous woman of God. You have given me so many special memories and always remind me of your love. You are my best friend and your advice never leaves my heart. My life is rich because you are with me. I love you.

To my father Jose Rosado, who reminded me of his love during hard- times. Thank you daddy for the moments you allow me to see your heart. I love you and I'm thankful for our special times together.

To my husband Carlos Rivera who loves, supports, encourages, and inspires me. You are the man I prayed for. I thank the Lord for uniting us in marriage. You have been a tremendous blessing to me. The Lord continues to use you to restore the broken places in my heart. Thank you for all the wonderful memories you have given our family. I look forward to a lifetime of love with you. You are a wonderful father, husband and my closest friend. You are my valiant, righteous man of God. You are my dance partner for life. You know I love to dance with you.

To my children who bring me joy each day. To my eldest, my soldier Glenn, continue to be the amazing person you are. Climb the highest mountain my son.

To my butterfly Denivia, you are my free spirit. You will touch many lives with your beautiful spirit.

To my brave athlete Ayden, you are the goodness in my heart. Your greatness comes from your compassion and kindness toward others.

You all have changed my life for the better. I love you all.

There are a host of family and friends that I haven't personally mentioned by name but I want you all to know I love and appreciate you. I would not be the person I am today without your contribution to my life.

~Table of Contents~

~Foreword~

I had the pleasure of meeting Alicia in 2011 at one of my conferences. The following year she hosted her first Dancing For Him conference in New York "Passionate," and began her first year in Dancing For Him Ministries' online school. She was an exemplary student who went above and beyond in her studies. She graduated from the school in 2014 and hosted her second DFH conference. What an anointed and wonderful dancer Alicia is, with such a heart and passion for the Lord! In addition to managing and choreographing for her own company, she is also a part of an amazing Christian dance company, Dance Ministry Institute that performs in New York and internationally. She established Jubilee Dance Studio Inc. in 2012 and teaches in a variety of settings. Alicia partners with other DFH students to serve the community. What a servant's heart she has. I am abundantly blessed to see how she and her various avenues of artistic ministry have grown since we first met.

As her 'dance Pastor,' I am so proud of what she has done with this book! It began as her final project for the DFH School. After reading the manuscript, I immediately suggested that she publish it as a book. I knew it would be a written work that would help and encourage many women who will have also gone through similar life issues. It is a story of her life's testimony, of how God stirred a passion in her to dance early in life. While unaware of God's plan for her life at that young age, she was already training to dance for the Lord. Along the way there were many trials. But that road led to Christ and her life's purpose. This story will encourage others to move forward in their talents and abilities to serve the Lord with kingdom purpose. Her testimony will give others hope that God will take you through the hard times and bring restoration through faith and obedience. Her prayer is also that her testimony will encourage anyone living in an abusive relationship to get out.

She is now a living witness that God answers prayers. He answered her prayer when she met her husband, Carlos (her Boaz). I know she prays that every reader will understand that salvation isn't freedom from trials but the assurance of everlasting life through faith in Jesus. The message in this book is likened to that of Jer. 29:11 God has a purpose and plan for us. In our life journey the Lord continuously reveals His purpose for us. I pray this book touches your life as it (and she) has mine.

Pastor Lynn M. Hayden
Dancing For Him Ministries

~Preface~

I started dancing at the age of 10 after watching Debbie Allen in "Fame." She was the first minority woman I'd seen who was successful and powerful. Growing up in the 1970s wasn't easy for minorities since the time period followed the assassination of Dr. Martin Luther King Jr. Representation of successful minorities was few and far between. All young people at some time or another identify with someone who inspires them to dream of great personal accomplishments. My dream wasn't to be rich or famous but to be accepted. I connected success with acceptance and acceptance with happiness.

I was driven to become the best dancer I could be and trained for many years with masters of the art. In my journey I discovered that success wasn't the key to happiness. As I continued to search for acceptance I made decisions that led to unfortunate events. God has always given me a way out and He will do the same for all who seek Him. It's important to remember you are not alone in your life journey.

"No temptation has overtaken you except what is common to mankind. And God is faithful; he will not let you be tempted beyond what you can bear. But when you are tempted, he will also provide a way out so that you can endure it" (1 Corinthians 10:13 NIV).

For many years I carried my memories as a heavy burden that weighed me down and left me feeling lost. When I accepted Jesus I found the acceptance and joy I longed for. As I studied the truth of God's word I found my identity and purpose. To see dance presented for the Lord in church was a pivotal time in my life. It was that moment the Lord revealed to me that He prepared me to serve Him with my skill as a dancer.

I was inexperienced in dancing for the Lord and in order to become more skilled in worship I entered school to study worship arts. The last school assignment in worship school prompted me to write this book. We were given a few options for a final assignment and one of them was to write a book. I selected the option of writing my testimony in the form of a book. There were many emotional moments as I recorded my memories and when I was finished my burden was lifted. I learned to appreciate my life trials as I recorded them, understanding—perhaps for the first time—that our troubles help to build character and draw us near to God.

"Therefore, since we have been justified through faith, we have peace with God through our Lord Jesus Christ, through whom we have gained access by faith into this grace in which we now stand. And we boast in the hope of the glory of God. Not only so, but we also glory in our sufferings, because we know that suffering produces perseverance; perseverance, character; and character, hope. And hope does not put us to shame, because God's love has been poured out into our hearts through the Holy Spirit, who has been given" (Romans 5:1-5 NIV).

I've been teaching for over 20 years and I'm always amazed at how a dance class can foster so many relationships and mentoring sessions. I've used my testimony as a tool to mentor and encourage others countless times over the years. It is my hope and prayer that as you read my testimony you will look to Jesus for the answers to your questions. I pray you are encouraged to pursue all that God has given you a passion to do and have faith that the Lord will bring you through failures. Victory is ours through faith in Jesus Christ who lived, died and resurrected for us. He gave us the Holy Spirit as our advocate and helper.

"If you love me, keep my commands. And I will ask the Father, and he will give you another advocate to help you and be with you forever—the Spirit of truth. The world cannot accept him, because it neither sees him nor knows him. But you know him, for he lives with you and will be in you. I will not leave you as orphans; I will come to you. Before long, the world will not see me anymore, but you will see me. Because I live, you also will live. On that day you will realize that I am in my Father, and you are in me, and I am in you. Whoever has my commands and keeps them is the one who loves me. The one who loves me will be loved by my Father, and I too will love them and show myself to them" (John 14:15-21 NIV).

Chapter 1

~A Happy Place~

I can't tell you the number of times I sat and listened as my mother recounted her childhood experiences. All of her stories kept me captivated and taught me valuable life lessons. The only differences in the stories she told in later years were the names of the players, but all were part of our one family line. One story she told of witnessing her father attacking her mother in a jealous rage, was told and retold in our family many times. Here's how my mother told it to me.

At a very young age my mother sat playing on the porch when she noticed the screen door of the house open and close. Thinking it was unusual that the door opened, she walked to the house and entered. She found her father under the dining table bending over her mother with a knife in hand. Her mother held his arm to prevent him from pushing the knife into her chest. She ran to her mother's side and grabbed the blade of the knife. Her father pleaded with her to let go but she held on, watching her mother bleed from her wounds. She was determined to stop her father's attack. The struggle ended with a sudden flash of light and loud pop. Her father crawled on the floor, bleeding from a bullet wound. His mother-in-law shot him to defend her eldest daughter from further harm and possible death.

I understood at a young age how precious life is from listening to family stories. I loved my grandmother and my mother and I

1

was so glad they survived the violence they once endured. Family stories were passed down from generation to generation, warning others of errors in decisions and the consequences. Our history was full of rape, incest, abuse, violence and death. Not much has changed in my lifetime. All the crimes of our ancestors were continued through my generation. We kept our family atrocities buried, but they resurfaced in ugly family disagreements. Siblings had arguments that sometimes ended in physical altercations, but they always stuck together to survive. It was like sitting in a lifeboat in the middle of an ocean full of sharks. If you stepped out, there was little chance of survival.

My personal story began when I learned my paternal grandparents rejected me as a baby because of my mother's ethnicity. Knowing this left me longing for their approval and feeling inferior because of my appearance. I knew they loved me and they treated me well but I was always listening for words that would label me as the undesired child. I grew close to my maternal relatives since I felt comfortable about my appearance in their presence.

My childhood home was always filled with music. My mother would sing and dance as she moved about, completing her household duties. When we visited relatives, there was always music, dancing, singing, and food. I watched and listened to our family and would pretend with my dolls to dance and sing in a happy life. We had good times as a family; however, there were bad times that would leave me feeling helpless and looking for an escape from unpleasant events.

Growing up in the 1970s was a challenge as a minority. My life experiences were limited to home and school. This was a decade where culture was still adjusting to the events of the 1960s, such as the race riots and the assassinations of John F. Kennedy and Martin Luther King. These leaders paved the way for the rights of minorities, but in the aftermath, social exclusion still existed among people, including my family.

I didn't fit in with any group at school, which added to my feelings of inferiority. I was ignored by most of my peers or treated unkindly. Most Caucasian children stayed together and tolerated my presence in play-groups but never really connected with me. Many of my African American peers rejected me, telling me I thought I was "better" because my skin was lighter. My Hispanic peers told me I was "fake" because I didn't speak Spanish. I felt unloved and ugly. I wished I could look different: hair, eyes, and skin.

"A cheerful heart is good medicine, but a crushed spirit dries up the bones" (Proverbs 17:22, NIV).

Much of the acceptance and love I received came from my extended family. My mother and her sisters raised all of their children together so my cousins were more like siblings living in different households. We were raised to love and defend each other against those who would try to harm us. We all had abusive or absentee fathers, so we didn't know what a father's love felt like. I knew my father as a selfish, prideful individual, but I still longed for his love. I heard my parents argue many times, ending as my father walked out. We sat with the echo of his hurtful words, wondering when and if he would return. I sat with an ache in my heart as I watched my mother cry in secret and hide her pain in my presence. I was angry with my father for causing her pain and sometimes prayed he would not return home. Why couldn't my father just be good and make her happy? There came a time when I didn't believe in happiness anymore. I didn't have a model of a happy family to see the difference between my life and one filled with joy. In my hopelessness, I questioned God. Why did God allow bad things to happen? Why didn't God give us a happy life? Was I destined to live a life of violence, abuse and pain? Didn't everyone have some good inside? In my limited understanding of life, I reasoned that I shouldn't have been born.

Abuse and violence were part of my normal existence and took root in my thoughts about my future. I invented ways to escape the turmoil that caused so much anxiety in my life. I needed to find a happy place where all was good in order to forget my suffering.

I immersed myself in music-performance television programs like *Soul Train, American Bandstand,* and *Solid Gold.* The people all looked happy and free no matter their ethnicity. I desired to live carefree like that. I impersonated people in the show, dancing and singing around my room. Play-acting was my way to dismiss dismal thoughts from my mind. I could fabricate a cheerful character but in the blink of an eye, my paradise evaporated at the sound of my parents fighting and my mother's sobs. Unease and sorrow crept back into my thoughts. Fear caused my heart to beat rapidly and I felt cold. My whole body would shake when I thought of losing my family. If I lost them I would be alone and there was little assurance of security.

At the age of ten, we took a family trip to visit with my mother's relatives in South Carolina. My mother's uncle packed us up in his car and drove for 14 hours from New York to our southern destination. The car was filled with chatter between the adults and children. I was excited because it would be my first time leaving New York and visiting my mother's birthplace. We arrived in the middle of the night and my aunt rushed to escort us to a bed to rest. The next day I went out and experienced the scorching southern temperature in August. I stayed in as much as possible after that experience to avoid the dry oppressive heat. At night, the temperature cooled enough to enjoy the sounds of the nearby forest and starry sky. All seemed to be going well between my parents and that gave me hope. We visited relatives and I frequently glanced at and listened to my parents, expecting them to erupt in an argument and ruin our vacation, but they seemed fine. When it was time to return home, we said goodbye to our family and once again piled into my uncle's car for our journey back to New York. Once we pulled off, I noticed an awkward silence. I eavesdropped on the adults speaking and heard my father ask my uncle to drive him to Maryland and leave him there to visit his own sister. My mother looked troubled. We left my father in Maryland and continued home. When we arrived home my mother told me my father wasn't coming back. I was in shock.

He left us to pursue a new life. I didn't realize it then, but this life-changing event would send me on a journey to search for a place to belong and my identity.

Without my father's income, my mother worked multiple jobs to pay the bills. Since my mother couldn't be home, I became a latchkey kid. I helped to care for my younger brother while my mother worked late hours. He was often sick and sometimes my mother would spend days traveling back and forth to the hospital to care for both of us. I stayed home alone or with family while my mother worked to support our family. The time I spent watching television increased to fill the hours of solitude. I missed my father, but I didn't want to go back to a destructive life. Memories of the storms with him overshadowed the good times.

Images of my father physically hurting my mother as she flailed her arms in defense haunted me. She hurt herself once when she was frustrated after an argument with my father. I hid as I watched, my heart pounding hard in my chest. I feared losing my mother; she was the only person who made me feel important and loved. She looked me in the eye when she talked to me and listened intently to every word I spoke. I admired her beauty, buried my face in her bosom and inhaled her sweetness every chance I could. She always made everything special even though we didn't have much. She filled my life with joy and I wanted to hear her laughter instead of sobs of pain. Where was her happy place? Could I find a way to make her happy?

My mother started reading the Bible and returned to church after she separated from my father. She shared Bible stories with me about the heroes of faith, Jesus and salvation. I saw a transformation in her as she studied God's word. I didn't understand why she was joyful, but I was grateful. It seemed life was looking better for us with her newfound faith.

"A father to the fatherless, a defender of widows, is God in His holy dwelling. God sets the lonely in families, he leads out the prisoners with singing; but the rebellious live in a sun-scorched land" (Psalms 68:5-6 NIV).

My mother continued to work long hours and I fell into a routine of school, home, homework and television. One night, I watched the movie Fame with Debbie Allen. She twirled, leaped and kicked her legs high with seemingly little effort, confidence and strength. What really got my attention was her appearance. I watched many television shows but this was the first time I noticed someone with similar physical features to myself, which inspired me. Many of the characters portrayed on television left me feeling hopeless, but this woman was a master of her craft. I decided I wanted to be a dancer. I worked hard to stretch so I could try to dance like my role model. I jumped and twirled, believing I looked like the dancers on television but I knew I needed training. I shared my passion with my mother and she enrolled me in dance school with her limited funds. I was excited about dance school and attended once per week. I wanted to train every day to be the best. I wanted to dance for life.

I was fortunate to have artistically gifted teachers in elementary school that used their talents to pour into their students. I was involved in choir and school plays that prepared me for my future as an artist. I learned hard lessons about giving your best no matter your role or emotions. When I worked with excellence I was given the best roles in school performances. I excelled in the performances and developed a passion for the arts.

Graduation was a big deal for me. Our class rehearsed hard to have the best graduation ceremony. My father came to my graduation with my mom. He'd already been gone from our lives for a full year and I could still see the pain in my mother's face when he visited. I sang and danced with energy and excitement. This was my day to shine. I looked forward to moving on to bigger and better places and I was eager to advance. After graduation, my parents wore proud smiles and rained kisses on me. I returned home elated about the day and started reading the comments in my autograph book. I found a priceless treasure in my book. My mother wrote a poem just for me.

To Alicia
From Mommy:

To love you before you were born
That love that never ends
To love you from a baby
Was that blessing heaven sends
To watch you take your first steps
Caused my heart to skip a beat
And the day you called me mommy
Made my life complete
The day you went to day care
You kicked and screamed and cried
The day you graduated there
The smile you wore was wide
Now those days are loving thoughts
And years have come to now
All your thoughts and hopes and dreams
Are crystalizing, how?
Because you're taking one more step
Towards another goal
And mommy will always be there
If you need a hand to hold
For I am very proud of you
And love you more each day
I want your dreams to all come true
In each and every way

Congratulations

Chapter 2

~New Status, Old Struggle~

Leaving elementary school was a scary and painful experience for me. After spending six years in a place where I knew everyone, it was hard to say goodbye. I was hopeful that I would get into a junior high school where I could be with my same classmates. Mark Twain Performing Arts School was conducting auditions and many of my friends were signed up to attend. I wanted to attend Mark Twain to continue my dance training, so I signed up to audition as well. The day of my audition, I froze during the drama portion. I quickly left the school feeling shame and never completed my audition. I waited for a reply from the school in hopes that they would accept me in spite of my failure to complete my audition. When the letter finally arrived, I looked at the envelope with my heart racing. I opened the letter and read slowly that I was rejected from the program. I felt a streak of cold fear and cried until my eyes were swollen. I fell into a deep depression in the days that followed. We were in the summer months with sunny skies and warm weather but I saw only darkness. I was placed by the state in a school with a poor reputation. It seemed like my life was over and I would never be able to accomplish my dream of becoming a dancer. I was doomed to live a troubled life inside the walls of our small apartment.

My mother was concerned about my sullen mood and took me shopping at the mall. We walked the mall, window-shopping when we bumped into my mother's good friend, Autumn. Autumn was battling a serious illness, but she never let it show in her countenance. I heard my mother talk with her sometimes about her battle, but she still praised God through her suffering. I stood staring in a store window as my mother shared her concern for me with Autumn. I felt so selfish hearing my own story and knowing how much greater Autumn suffered, yet in silence. I expected to hear both my mother and Autumn tell me to be grateful, but instead they shared something I didn't expect. With love and gentleness in her eyes and voice, Autumn shared the Gospel of Christ and salvation with me. I remembered my mom explaining the Gospel to me before, but this time my heart was ready. I accepted Jesus and Autumn gave me a Bible and I recorded the date on the first page. She told me I was saved. I didn't understand the meaning of being saved, but it sounded good and I felt comforted and at peace. I felt like my new status would somehow end rejection and protect me from harm. I accepted my new status and prepared to step on fresh ground in a new school.

"For whosoever shall call upon the name of the Lord shall be saved" (Romans 10:13 KJV).

I began my first day of junior high feeling both dread and fear of transitioning into a new environment. I boarded the bus with other students from my neighborhood. I recognized some of the students but there were others I'd never met before. When our school bus pulled up to the school, my fears were intensified at the sight of people protesting our arrival. Our group was made up of students of various ethnic backgrounds and we were in a predominately Caucasian neighborhood where racial tension was high. The protesters were a small group of residents who were not in agreement with our group attending the neighborhood school. They stood outside the school with their faces painted half black and half white, yelling at us to go home. I'd never experienced this before and I wondered if I could survive in this school. I remembered my new status as "saved" and wondered why God would send me into this. I didn't want to face prejudice anymore. It would be easier if I were born with light skin and straight hair. I felt cursed. My goal was still to work hard enough so I could become a dancer on television like Debbie Allen and be happy.

The first half of the day seemed to go on forever. When the lunch bell rang I followed all the other students down to the cafeteria still feeling lost. There were crowds of students talking and laughing as they ate. I moved through the line with my tray and looked around for a seat. I started to sit at the end of the lunch table away from all the other students when I caught a glimpse of a hand waving at me. I looked again and there was a brown-haired girl waving and patting the spot next to her. Was this a joke? I walked over and she invited me to sit next to her. I sat and she asked my name and introduced herself as Pamela. She said I looked sad and asked me so many questions about myself that we talked until the end of lunch. She was the only person to reach out to me that first day, but it gave me hope. We became close and did everything together: choir, band, sleepovers and hour-long phone chats. She even wrote to me in the summer from sleep away camp. She took care to write her letters in her best handwriting on beautiful stationary with stickers. Finally I had someone I could call a true friend. I looked forward to school each day just to spend time with my best friend. Every day was an adventure with Pam.

As the months passed I found myself missing dance and feeling anxious about my future. There weren't any dance programs in my new school, just dodge ball. I kept myself in shape attending track and field and cheerleading at a neighborhood community center. I was determined to get back into dancing. I set a goal to graduate early so I could attend a performing arts high school where I could continue my dance training.

In 8th grade, I auditioned for 3 schools and was accepted into John Dewey High School. I would be graduating a year ahead of my class, but I was happy that I would be leaving that dreadful school. I would miss Pamela, but we promised to keep in touch. She would apply to my school next year and if accepted, she would attend my school the following year. I was excited about entering high school. I dreamed of dancing on lunchroom tables and in the halls like the actors in the show "Fame." Finally I would be in a place where I belonged and move forward in my dance training. Now my life as a dancer would begin.

I entered high school with anticipation of a new freedom and acceptance by my peers. The first few weeks were discouraging, because I was scheduled to take a weight lifting class instead of dance. School policy stated that freshman couldn't participate in dance. I would be stuck in weight training or basketball for an entire year. I was tired of waiting. If I couldn't dance this year then I wouldn't attend any physical education class. I skipped every weight lifting class for weeks. I knew this was a bad decision but I didn't care if I failed. My excessive absence in gym landed me right in the dean's office. I explained to the dean why I wouldn't go to class and he walked me over to the dance instructor after our meeting. To my surprise he asked the dance instructor if I could participate in class as a trial. If I did well the dean would authorize my registration in dance. The dance instructor was a man by the name of John M. Goring. He flashed a smile at me and agreed to allow me in his dance class program. I was so happy and yet nervous. I thanked the dean with my heart beating hard and returned home filled with renewed hope.

My first day of class was just a taste of the hard work I would experience in my training. Our classes were 1-2 hours of barre and floor work with choreography. I worked hard but was often frustrated that I couldn't execute movement like the more experienced dancers. I was allowed to stay in the dance class permanently and Mr. Goring invited me to become a member of the dance ensemble. In dance ensemble the dancers were required to stay after school 2-3 hours for dance rehearsal in addition to our day classes. I returned home late every day to complete homework and collapse from exhaustion, but I refused to give up. I thought I was prepared for a higher level of training, but my limited experience was poor preparation for the formal training I was receiving at that time. The movements professional dancers executed on television are far more difficult than they look.

Warm-ups were boring to me. If it were up to me I would skip warm-up and go straight to choreography. As I trained, I learned how warm-ups train our bodies to be strong, flexible and help with good balance. I was encouraged by my progression in dance technique. I was confident that if I worked hard and remained committed to my training I could work as a professional dancer.

Mr. Goring shared stories of his professional dance career. He would preface many of his lessons with "in the professional world" to get his point across about discipline. He explained why working hard was important to build strength and skill level to dance with excellence. I appreciated all the hard work he put into our training, but he was strict. If any of us displeased him he would yell and sometimes throw us out of the dance studio. I was thrown out once for not dancing with enough passion. I cried until I felt like I didn't have any tears left. I became accustomed to the occasional dance class conflicts and grew indifferent. The passion to dance was more powerful than any offense. Thankfully we had a second dance instructor, Ms. Russell, who was the voice of reason. She would resolve many of the conflicts we had with a quiet word to the parties involved. Ms. Russell worked closely with Mr. Goring all year to train and mentor dance students. It created a nice balance to have a male and female team. Ms.

Russell taught modern dance Graham technique with passion. I loved Graham technique because of its expressive movement. Modern dance gives the freedom to step out of the "ballet box" and choreography movement that expresses emotion with the face and body. Twists and turns of spirals and deep curves in contractions allow the body to rise, fall and make shapes unseen in ballet.

Mr. Goring taught ballet, jazz and Afro-Caribbean. I enjoyed jazz since it was upbeat and fun to dance to the popular music I listened to. Afro-Caribbean is high energy, polycentric dance movement performed with polyrhythmic music accompaniment. I learned to isolate arms, legs, head and torso movement to different rhythms simultaneously. It was challenging to learn this form of dance, but I learned that it builds coordination and the ability to hear and dance to different rhythms in music.

The dance ensemble trained all year for various performance events in school. I enjoyed the year-end performance because students were given the opportunity to choreograph a work and perform it. My first work was a duet that I co-choreographed and danced with a friend named Christian. Partnering can be easy or hard depending on the chemistry between the two dancers. Christian and I had great chemistry and we were always paired together for partnering work. Whenever we were given choreography we were able to execute it with ease because we knew each other so well. I had bad experiences with partners with whom I had negative chemistry. Once I was paired with a gentleman who threw me off his shoulders in anger when we disagreed about a dance lift. I hit the floor hard to the shock of the choreographer who was unaware of the squabble. The problem was overlooked and I danced with my partner with heavy tension between us. My desire to dance was so great that the argument didn't matter. I stayed in character and gave my best on stage.

I enrolled in an acting class to improve my performance skills. I enjoyed taking on another personality on stage and I desired to be more skillful. It's important to study the character you will portray and meditate on the possible thoughts and feelings of that character. In the same way, dancing as a specific character or to the emotion of a song involves the same meditation. Expressive dance can be used to communicate a story or message through movement. Often the words of a song expressed my true emotions of sadness and rejection. The longing to feel accepted and loved was never far from my heart. Dancing allowed me to release everything I couldn't verbalize. I purposely chose songs that expressed my struggle and danced from the deepest part of my soul. Every day I looked in the mirror and disliked my own image. I struggled with my identity and was confused about my purpose. Why was I born? Why was God allowing me to suffer?

"And we know that all things work together for good to them that love God, to them who are the called according to his purpose" (Romans 8:28 KJV).

I watched with jealousy as my dance peers with skills more advanced than my own were cast in lead roles. I pushed myself harder to get noticed by choreographers and sulked when I was overlooked. Pride crept in and I was not above being cruel to others in my envy. My teacher gave me the opportunity to set choreography on my class and I was excited to be acknowledged. Finally I would have a chance to display my skills. I started my choreography with 20 people in a jazz combination but quickly realized the difficulty of working with a large group. I worked hard to include different entrances and exits for various groups and midway hit a wall. The last few rehearsals were very close to the performance date and the dancers who were excited in the beginning looked tired and frustrated since I hadn't finished the choreography. I felt every eye on me and I wondered if they doubted my ability. Mr. Goring gave me a deadline to finish and warned that if I missed it, he would cut the dance. I finished on time and I was proud, but I felt a change in me that wasn't good. Pride, envy and selfish ambition unexpectedly swelled up in my heart and scared me. I was focused on my own personal fame and felt as though I would do anything to make my dreams come true. I knew my thoughts and feelings were not truly part of who I really was deep inside.

"In his pride the wicked man does not seek him; in all his thoughts there is no room for God" (Psalms 10:4 NIV).

Chapter 3

~*Goodbye Innocence*~

The first two years of high school, I fell prey to peer pressure. Everyone was "going steady" but I could only watch from a distance. I was inexperienced with relationships, so I was curious and nervous about getting close to the opposite sex. I wasn't dating and felt lonely. I was usually the third wheel with my group of friends. I waited as couples dipped in and out of dark places to steal a private moment. They were sexually active and tried to convince me to try it too, but I wanted to remain pure for my wedding day. When I accepted Jesus, I was told I was saved and I didn't want to lose that status. I still didn't understand what it meant to be saved, but I knew my friends were crossing lines they shouldn't be crossing. I didn't share my belief because I thought everyone would laugh at me. I didn't know anyone else who was bragging about being saved. I lost sleep thinking, reasoning and doubting what was right and wrong.

I started dating the first boy who showed interest out of desperation to fit in. He continually pressured me for sex. He went as far as asking my friends to talk me into giving in to him. I listened to everyone tell me "grow up" and "everyone does it." Eventually I broke down and gave in. I had no idea what to do or expect but I didn't like the experience. All I could think of was that God saw me. I was tainted, and not worth marrying. I was left with shame, guilt and sadness. The relationship turned abusive and ended fast, leaving me heartbroken. As I searched for a prince, I ended up involved in more abusive relationships. I was falling deeper into darkness. I never shared my pain with anyone, not even my best friend. I was too embarrassed and afraid of being judged by others.

I started taking walks alone on the beach near my home to talk to God. I asked Him to send me my knight in shining armor. I asked for someone who would be loving, kind, responsible, handsome and love me as I am. I wanted my prince to come and end my loneliness and suffering. I was desperate to meet him, fall in love and get married. He would take me away from all the sadness and we would live happy together. Could I live happily ever after like the fairy tales told? I didn't know anyone who lived that way.

> "Daughters of Jerusalem, I charge you by the gazelles and by the does of the field: Do not arouse or awaken love until it so desires" (Song of Solomon 2:7 NIV).

Just before my 16th birthday I met a young man named Glenn. We had fun going out together and he gave me lots of nice gifts. None of the other boys took me out or gave me gifts. I felt appreciated and pretty. I didn't want to be alone anymore and this new attention gave me hope of finding happiness. I was determined this relationship would last. I had to be careful not to do anything that would make him leave me or hurt me. I believed I was responsible for all the failed relationships. It was my fault that these young men abused me. I had to fix myself so I could be loved. I wanted to be married so my shame would disappear.

I learned things about Glenn that I could relate to. He grew up without his father. His father died when he was just a baby. Though I grew up with my father for part of my life, I understood the feeling of having an absent father. Glenn believed he would have the same fate as his father and die young. This stirred my compassion and I encouraged him to believe for a better future for himself. He lived a criminal lifestyle to survive. From a young age he and his brothers would steal from delivery trucks to have food to eat. Surviving poverty had been a constant battle for his family as well as my own, but we used different methods of obtaining basic needs. Even though he wasn't perfect I thought I could change him over time. I knew if he continued living a criminal life he would end up in jail or dead. I started working my first job and purchased food for him so he would possibly follow my lead and get a job. We had endless arguments about living an honest life, but he continued to live a criminal lifestyle. Painful memories came to haunt me as he became abusive toward me. By now I believed this was normal in relationships. I saw it with my parents and it's all I'd ever known in my own relationships. I tolerated the abuse and assumed it would stop when his love for me grew stronger but instead the abuse intensified.

I learned that Glenn had an addiction to drugs. He was a master at hiding his habit but eventually I discovered his secret. When he was under the influence he was a different person and I suffered the effects of his highs and lows on drugs. I tried to avoid abuse by humbling myself but violence was inevitable in a relationship with a drug addict. He was unreasonably jealous with a strong suspicion that I would get involved with another man. Most of our arguments sparked from his paranoia of my looking in the direction of a man. If I walked away from a disagreement in anger there was a price to pay.

Sometimes I felt my feet leave the ground and my air cut off from a choke-hold. I didn't have time to react before blacking out. I didn't expect to awaken from this quick sleep nor did I care. I welcomed the darkness over having my face squeezed until my teeth cut into my cheeks, or hear his accusations and see him stare at me with disgust. Dance was my outlet during my suffering. I danced through every verbal insult and unwelcomed physical invasion that left scars inside and out. Pain was always there to greet me when my dancing ceased.

"Wrath is cruel, anger is overwhelming, but who can stand before jealousy" (Proverbs 27:4 NIV)?

Junior and senior year I participated in college courses for high school students at Brooklyn College and Borough of Manhattan Community College. Mr. Goring and Ms. Russell arranged classes for ensemble members with professional dancers outside of school. We were exposed to Alvin Ailey, Eleo Pomare, June Lewis and John Parks. My dreams of dancing professionally were finally crystallizing, but I was so distracted by my inner suffering, I couldn't appreciate the progress toward my goals.

I'd grown accustomed to walking with my eyes downcast to avoid looking at anyone. I didn't want to be accused or found guilty of desiring another man. Glenn believed that I looked at other men's bodies in dance class and would eventually be unfaithful to him. He frequently asked if I changed my clothing in the same room with men and when I denied it he looked at me with distrust. Dance was my passion but how could I continue to dance with Glenn's jealousy looming over me like a dark cloud? I sank deeper into hopelessness each day. Relief came during the times I turned on music and began spinning and leaping. When I danced, I became someone else. I lived in my own world, moving freely to music. I spent hours in dance studios training and rehearsing for auditions. I didn't want to return home where loneliness, abuse and pain lived. My exposure to the professional world at a young age opened my eyes to the snares that waited to catch naïve artists looking for fame. Most of the time I could see the traps that many young girls would fall into but I was also taken advantage of from time to time. There were times I paid for pictures only to return to a vacant room with no trace of the company in its former space. Many dance auditions turned out to be jobs for strippers and other X-rated positions. It was discouraging to find out so many companies were preying on the young to make money. I auditioned for York Productions at age 16 and was offered a part as a backup singer/dancer. The producer named the group "Hot" and recorded 3 songs and videos. We appeared on television a few times so I thought I had my big break. The producer took the group out to eat to discuss future promotions and spent hundreds of dollars on new clothes for us to look nice for performances. The producer owned and operated his own recording studio in his home where we spent hours recording and rehearsing. His home was more like a mansion with many rooms, all with fancy décor.

Some of the other girls in the group started to talk among themselves about things that happened in the mansion. I started to ask questions and found out they were intimate with either the producer or his assistant. One of the girls shyly told me she wanted to be one of the wives of the producer and told me he was interested in having me as a wife too. He had many wives and followers that worked for him and invested money into his business. There were hundreds of them in the community. Naturally I was concerned because I signed a legal contract with this company. If I left, I was afraid they would sue me. I was so close to my dream but I didn't want to become someone's wife at 16 years old. I timidly asked the producer to be released from the contract and he agreed. He gave me a large sum of money as compensation along with my contract to destroy. He also gave me photos he had of me from a photo shoot but kept one picture. I thought it was odd for him to keep my photo but left in a hurry.

As I traveled home I decided I would stop in to visit Glenn. When I arrived at his door he came out of the house instead of inviting me in. Behind him I could see another girl and I pushed past him to enter. My eyes quickly scanned the room to see our photos ripped down from the walls. It must have been done in a hurry because the corners of the photos were still taped to the wall. She sat looking confidently at me while caressing her long black hair. I was devastated and left feeling like my heart had been ripped out and trampled. I tried to be everything he wanted me to be so he would be happy. How could he do this to me? I couldn't eat, sleep or stop trembling. A friend offered me her sleeping pills to help me relax and sleep better.

A few days later, I returned to confront him. He said so many hurtful things that left me feeling worthless. I took the sleeping pills my friend gave me and swallowed them all. I wanted to sleep forever. He called me crazy and dialed EMS. At the hospital I was forced to drink something to make me vomit and absorb the poison. As I lay on the hospital bed, I stared at a clock on the wall in front of me and became drowsy. My heart raced in my chest and I couldn't breathe. *So this is how I will die,* I thought, *full of fear and regret.* I didn't want to die and silently prayed to God, asking him to spare my life. I wanted to see my family and enjoy life. I vowed I would never try to take my life again. My life was not mine to take.

> *"Do you not know that your bodies are temples of the Holy Spirit, who is in you, whom you have received from God? You are not your own; you were bought at a price. Therefore honor God with your bodies"* (1 Corinthians 6:19-20 NIV).

After I was released from the hospital I sat through many conversations with concerned family members. My father spent time with me too. It was nice to feel loved by my family but I was concerned about my mother. She didn't speak much about what happened and seemed angry. I was ashamed of what I had done. I finally understood how selfish my suicide attempt was. How could I put my mother through this when she had suffered so much? I returned to school on my best behavior in an effort to reconcile with my mom. I was required to meet with a psychiatrist every week for counseling. I was bored and unresponsive at first but noticed it only increased the interest of the doctor. I used my acting skills to appear happy in counseling. I must have been convincing since the psychiatrist closed my case. I still carried a heavy sadness but I was relieved the drilling sessions were over. I didn't want anyone asking me questions about my life. I was too ashamed to share all of my bad decisions. I just wanted to focus on finishing high school and preparing for graduation. I danced every chance I could to get me through the year until the end of high school.

I prepared all year for the annual dance ensemble production. This would be my last time dancing in high school. I would say goodbye to many dear friends and teachers. I loved them and shared so much with them throughout the years. This was a place where I felt accepted and loved. I would miss everyone. It was customary for senior level dancers to dance a solo for the show. I would dance to the song "Got to be There" by Chaka Khan. I invited Glenn to come to the show and he agreed. He would see me dance and I hoped he would see my passion and love me for who I was. I hoped his jealousy about my dancing would cease. I told him I would dedicate the song to him as I danced. Truth is I wasn't sure I danced for him.

My father would be there along with my mother and a host of family members. I wanted to restore relationships torn by my disobedience and selfishness. I thought about everyone who would watch me and see how I'd grown over the years. Would they be proud when the music stopped? I danced with passion and strength to capture the audience. I was focused on executing each movement and transition just as I had been instructed. The entire experience with costume changes, makeup, entrances and exits on stage, lights and dancing with all the ensemble members that had become like family passed in a blink. After the finale, I was drenched with sweat and gasping for air. There was loud applause for the entire ensemble as we stood together to take a bow. The curtain closed and I was overwhelmed with all I'd accomplished and feared. I wondered if the world would welcome or reject me. It was time for me to move forward into unfamiliar territory and an uncertain future.

I didn't enter college right away after high school. I started working full time as a cosmetician during the day and a part time dancer during my off days and evenings. My mother purchased a house and moved all of us to a different nearby city. She was in a relationship with someone and he moved in our new home as well. It was weird for me to have a man other than my father in our home, but I was happy that she'd found someone to spend her life with. I reconciled with Glenn on his promise that our relationship would improve. We saw less of each other when I moved. The long distance between us stirred paranoid suspicion in him again. He returned to the angry tantrums and accused me of unfaithful behavior. He started appearing unexpectedly in places where he knew I would be. I traveled each day looking over my shoulder wondering if he would show up on the train or bus with his angry stare. I felt guilty even though I didn't have a reason. I was becoming paranoid just like Glenn.

I arrived at work most days shaking and crying after an argument with him. My supervisors and co-workers tried to comfort me but I dismissed them. I hid my life as best I could from everyone I knew. My problems were mine alone but it was an overwhelming burden to carry. Eventually I lost my job because of my mood swings and poor attendance.

I decided it was time for college. A new setting would give me new hope.

I attended a community college in lower Manhattan where I met wonderful professors who nurtured me and helped me gain employment with many professional modern dance companies and notable choreographers. Despite my emotional turmoil, I completed two years of college on the dean's list with honors, and was elected president of a dance club. I worked part-time in retail during the day and continued to dance nights and weekends. Work and school kept me away from home most of the day and night. Keeping busy was my way to avoid trouble and suppress anguish.

I left college when my mother was seriously injured in a car accident. She'd paid all my expenses in college and couldn't afford to continue since she was out of work. My tuition for college was too much for me with my small income. I continued to work with dance companies and part-time retail jobs, hoping to become more independent. Working and training with seasoned professional dancers helped me to advance to higher levels in dance technique, choreography and teaching. I enjoyed the challenge of learning different dance techniques and styles. I developed a new appreciation for the creativity and skill of the artistic directors. I danced to music that I'd never heard before and sometimes no music at all.

I discovered the art of dance is much deeper than simply moving to music. It is a personal expression of ideas, concepts, emotions and stories. Choreographers are inspired by anything they experience not just the words of a song. I looked at the world through a dancer's eyes. I saw movement in everything. I imagined myself dancing to the sound of ocean waves or sounds on a subway train. I watched the birds fly and thought how wonderful to sail through the air. I wondered if the feeling I experienced with leaps and turns was similar to that of birds flying.

I took the liberty of arriving to work early to stretch and have time to try some of my ideas before the other company members arrived at the studio. I felt peace when I danced alone. It felt as if a shroud of protection was around me. Why couldn't I feel the same peace at home? I hurried to my room and closed my bedroom door each time I returned home. On the other side of my closed door was trouble waiting.

The addition of a new personality to our family was a difficult adjustment. My mother's significant other had an overbearing nature that caused conflict in our family. I avoided him to keep peace, but storms were inevitable. Each time I returned home an argument ensued. This man wasn't my father nor did he treat me like a daughter. He made demands of me and criticized me, calling me names that crushed my heart. Abuse followed me everywhere. I craved love from my father but he wasn't around. I missed him. He had his own life now, married with a young son. When I visited him there was a distance between us. I needed his protection and affirmation. I needed his advice and comfort. I was caught in a whirlwind of conflict and confusion. I caused most arguments at home with my rebelliousness. An adult child living at home with a parent in a new relationship was not healthy. I needed to leave my mother's home so she could live trouble free.

I wanted my own home and family but financially I couldn't support myself. I reasoned that living in the same household and married to Glenn would stop his daily jealous accusations. I reasoned in my own ignorance that if he was aware of my whereabouts he could learn to trust and love me. I hastily made arrangements to register for a marriage license and we secretly married. I mailed out our paperwork and checked the mail daily for our certificate of marriage. Once I had the certificate in hand I gave my husband a copy as if this would prove my loyalty and end jealous conflicts. I held on to my secret for four months before I revealed our marriage to my mother. I moved into Glenn's apartment to begin our life together. I felt like a disruption in his routine instead of a welcomed companion. I was driven by pure emotion and deep inside I knew I had made a poor decision.

"For lack of guidance a nation falls, but victory is won through many advisers" (Proverbs 11:14 NIV).

Chapter 4

~Lost Passion~

Months passed and hopelessness filled my heart. I spent most of my days working and rehearsing late hours just to come home to a husband high on drugs or missing. He experimented with many different drugs to stimulate a new high. After a night of binging on PCP and sometimes crack cocaine, he returned home violent and paranoid. The nauseating sweetness of the chemicals he used permeated his body. I spent many nights either worried about him or fighting him off.

Dance was like a drug to make me feel good but it soon became ineffective. I remember as I stood many times before an audience's loud applause, I wondered why I continued to dance. I worked hard for acceptance based on performance and tried to carve out my own destiny. The result of my actions ended in grief and regret. The burning passion and desire to dance I once had dwindled to smoking remnants in a pit of ash. My life lacked purpose. At rehearsals, I moved through space in a trance, barely listening to the music. My counts were off and I couldn't remember choreography. I was consumed with despair. The director approached me with anger. He stepped close and looked into my eyes as he said, "You are not gifted. You have talent. You must work hard to be excellent."

His unforgettable statement left me confused and hurt. My sullen mood affected my appetite and I grew thin. My small frame gave me the appearance of a 12-year-old child. Friends frequently asked about my mood but it caused me to become more withdrawn. My heart was empty and I hid from everyone. I carried shame and guilt because of my abused life. I believed all that I suffered was my fault. I'd failed as a daughter, wife and a dancer. Eventually, I abandoned my job as a professional company dancer. I didn't see a reason to remain if I didn't have a gift to dance. I refused to return calls from concerned friends and directors. I kept my routine schedule to leave each day, pretending to go to work to get away from my husband. I spent hours in public places like libraries, parks and restaurants to clear my mind and consider my next step. I decided to spend more time with my husband and help him stay sober. I wanted to mend our marriage. I pushed myself to be my best in dance but not in my personal life. I knew I would miss the stage but I found other ways to keep dance in my life. At home, I played music and danced alone or walked to the beach and danced to the sounds of the waves. I continued to teach children and women but I no longer desired to perform. All I had left of my professional dance career were a few photos, playbills, posters and my memories. When I thought of what I had given up, a panic stirred in my chest. How could I give up my passion? What would I do with my life?

"Woe unto them that are wise in their own eyes, and prudent in their own sight" (Isaiah 5:21 KJV)!

I started a full time day job in sales to help support my family. I enjoyed teaching dance part time. I still worked long hours and I couldn't spend the time I thought I would with my husband. He continued to drift and eventually was unfaithful again. His affair continued long term. I was left feeling worthless. When I looked at him I could see he didn't care for me. He often told me that I was a good woman and I should leave him, but I stayed. He told me we didn't belong together because of our different ethnicities, but I stayed. I remained mostly because I didn't believe anyone else would want me. I would end up in a relationship just like this one again. Why start over again? A happy marriage was like a mythological tale. Happy marriage stories were great but nothing I could believe without witnessing a joyful married couple. If I left my husband, I would be forced to depend on my family to care for me again. I wanted to remain independent. I accepted any small displays of affection from my husband, but I felt my heart grow numb and cold. I didn't feel comfortable showing affection anymore. I couldn't speak to people or look at them. I lived in my own mind where I felt safe.

"Whoever conceals their sins does not prosper, but the one who confesses and renounces them finds mercy. Blessed is the one who always trembles before God, but whoever hardens their heart falls into trouble" (Proverbs 28:13-14 NIV).

~Familiar Feelings~

A year passed and my life with my husband grew distant. I exhausted every idea to build a good life with him, but I couldn't change him. I was tired and I didn't like my husband anymore. I thought about leaving and starting a new life away from him. I felt different now, stronger than before. I also felt sick with the thought of being alone. My perspective changed but that wasn't the only change in me. I noticed familiar changes in my body. I experienced similar changes 5 years prior when I became pregnant. I will never forget the fear I experienced after the doctor confirmed my first pregnancy. She must have noticed my stress and asked if I would terminate. I couldn't give an immediate answer so I left. I shared my news with friends and asked advice. Everyone suggested termination. I didn't come to a definite decision until weeks later. I made an appointment to terminate and thought about canceling many times, but I had Glenn urging me to go forward. He expressed his fear that the baby would be born with defects because of his drug habit. I decided to go forward in agreement with Glenn. The dreaded day of my appointment, I could barely stop shaking from fear. I clumsily dressed and left to meet Glenn. We traveled to the clinic and were greeted by protesters at the entrance. My fear increased as I sat through films and counseling. Doctors conducted tests to determine how many weeks gestation I was and looked at me concerned. They allowed me to listen to my baby's heartbeat before they handed me papers to sign away my baby's life. Everything inside of me wanted to run out of the clinic but I didn't. I signed all the consent papers and waited to be called. When my name was called, I was led into a room and asked to lie on a table while given anesthesia. I remember so many people working around me before passing into darkness. Glenn was left to wait outside during the procedure. I was nudged awake by a nurse and led to walk to the recovery room until the effects of the anesthesia subsided. She casually informed me of the sex of my baby, blood type and how many weeks gestation I was at the time. I sat for nearly an hour in the company of other women and cried from the deepest part of my soul. How could I murder my baby? I vowed to never terminate another pregnancy.

So here I was 5 years later with the familiar physical changes and familiar fears. I needed confirmation that I was indeed pregnant again. I called and made an appointment to get tested. I mentioned my suspicions to my husband and he seemed disinterested and uncaring. I told him I wouldn't terminate if I was pregnant and still he gave no response. As I turned to leave, I looked at him and he glared at me with a smirk. He was high again and probably waiting for me to leave so he could take more drugs. I turned and left without a second glance.

LOST PASSION

The testing was fast and the doctor confirmed what I already knew. I was pregnant and dreaded sharing the news with my husband. I returned home and delivered the news to Glenn but I wasn't greeted with a happy response. I longed to hear my husband tell me he looked forward to our new arrival but my words fell to the ground. He didn't respond to my statement but begged me to come closer with a lustful look. I refused with the excuse of work and started to iron my clothing but he repeatedly called me. He was angered by my rejection and approached me with clenched teeth. I shielded myself by holding the hot iron out in front of me to keep him away but he grabbed me. I used the iron to burn him so I could run out the door but he snatched me by the hair, lifted me and carried me back to our bedroom. I kicked and screamed to get away as he tore my clothing off. I pounded him with my fists but he was too strong. He wrapped his hands around my throat and lifted me from the bed. I clawed at his hands to free myself but it made him furious and he threw me toward our 9th floor window. I saw myself getting closer to the window and time seemed to slow down. I closed my eyes expecting a long fall to my death but hit the wall below the window and slid to the floor with a thud.

Before I could recover, he was above me lifting me by my neck again and slamming me down on the bed still clutching my throat. I strained my voice through gasps and begged him to let me go so I could call in late for work. He paused in thought then reluctantly released his grip. I sat up holding my neck. I was hurting all over and my neck burned. I walked over to the phone and turned my back to block his view while I dialed for help. I only had a few seconds to think. I wouldn't have enough time to give an address to authorities so I dialed family that lived close. I heard the phone ring and my heart started to race. My aunt answered and I screamed all the information I could before Glenn grabbed the phone. I held on to the phone and continued to scream.

DANCING IN SPIRIT AND TRUTH

We wrestled on the floor, but I was no match for his strength. He slammed the phone down on the cradle and continued to restrain me. The phone rang and he yanked it from the wall with one hand as he sat on me. I could only guess that my aunt was calling back to check on me. I hoped she would call the police so they would rescue me before Glenn killed me. I pushed at his face with my hands to try and free myself from his constraint but he straddled me on the floor. I wasn't strong enough to free myself. I exhausted myself and cried with a limp body. He stood up and stepped over me with a mumble. He looked around the room with a deranged expression then left abruptly. I slowly stepped out of the room and listened for movement. When I was sure he was gone I quickly locked the door. I could hear the sound of police sirens from the window. I ran to grab something to cover myself, but I barely had time before they knocked and announced their arrival. I grabbed a sheet to cover myself and opened the door quickly. I invited them in and they walked through the entire apartment as they questioned me. After they wrote a report of my story they advised me to leave immediately. I called my mother and asked to come home. She told me yes without pause. The police remained until my family arrived to help me gather my belongings.

~Back Home~

I returned to my mother's home ashamed and afraid of what I would face. I was prepared to do whatever she needed so that I could remain. She welcomed me in with love and compassion just like the story of the prodigal son. I heard her react with sighs as I recounted my story of abuse to the police. My mom clenched her hands tightly with her eyebrows knitted together and her mouth stretched tight. Every reaction told me she knew what I'd experienced and didn't want me to suffer the way she did. Now I understood her struggles with my father. I had my own struggles to fight through but I was grateful to have my mother to help me. I had a host of family members who were ready to step in and help me. I wondered why I had suffered so long in secret when help was only a phone call away. I wouldn't suffer in secret anymore.

A few days after the interview, the detectives called to inform me that my husband had been arrested on an unrelated charge. They asked if I was ready to press charges but I declined. I didn't want to face him. I just wanted to be safe and focus on my baby. Glenn was sent to a drug rehabilitation program instead of jail. It was a huge relief knowing he was off the streets and receiving treatment for addiction. It would give me time to sort out my life and thoughts. I had a precious baby for whom I would provide and live. I would never leave or hurt my child. I didn't have clear vision for the future but I knew I would love and cherish my baby for life.

Every day I prayed for a healthy baby. My family called me often to ask about my health and sent many gifts. My close cousin, Charrisse went to most doctor appointments with me. She was always there for me as the sister I never had. She listened to me pour out my heart about every broken dream and uncertain plans. I was grateful to have her, my mother, aunts and grandmothers who nurtured me and encouraged me during my pregnancy. I wondered each day that passed how my baby was growing. I loved feeling the little kicks and bumps in my belly. It was a sure sign of life growing within me. I didn't know if I was expecting a boy or a girl but it didn't matter. I loved my baby and looked forward to a joyful arrival.

After four months in rehabilitation my husband called to tell me he had been released and was ready to be a father. I felt uncomfortable and unsure of his sincerity but he assured me he was sober and wanted to repair our marriage. I decided to give him a chance, but I remained on guard. My mother's boyfriend, Chris offered to rent us his home located around the corner from my mother's home. I accepted the opportunity with the comfort that my mother was near just in case my husband relapsed.

As my pregnancy progressed I started having complications and was forced to stop working. My husband worked to take care of our expenses as we awaited the birth of our child. My condition worsened so my doctor scheduled labor induction. My doctor met me during check-in at the hospital and explained the induction procedure. Everything seemed simple and I expected an easy delivery. After the doctor ruptured my amniotic sac she looked concerned. I watched her walk to the door to speak with the nurse, then she left the room. The nurse asked me to walk with her to another room for a sonogram. Naturally I was concerned and asked questions. She just smiled and said the doctor was waiting for me. My doctor met me at the door and asked me to lie on the exam table as she rushed around to prep for the sonogram. She explained that very little amniotic fluid expelled and she wanted to check the baby.

My heart began to pound hard as she examined me. My eyes never left her face as I searched for her expression that would either calm or confirm my fears. I prayed silently for my baby to be ok. I couldn't lose the hope that had kept me all this time. My hope was to have a baby to love and cherish. Her expression changed to shock, then without a word I knew she had made a decision on what needed to be done. She explained that my amniotic fluid must have been leaking and I was left with very little fluid. She also discovered my baby was breach and I would need to have an emergency C-section to deliver. By now contractions were setting in and I was left to wait until a room was ready for me to deliver my baby.

The contractions were like no other pain I'd ever experienced. I felt as if I were being crushed and pulled apart at the same time. After five hours, my son Glenn Christian was delivered. I marveled at how wonderful he was. He was small but full of energy. I felt immense pain from the delivery but I was in awe of my little miracle. Looking at my son's little face filled me with a love I'd never felt before. My cold heart was resuscitated at the sight of my precious son. I held him close, inhaled his scent and kissed him repeatedly. Here was a tiny person that depended on me to care for him. I vowed to give him the best life I could.

I struggled to care for my little boy each day with the help of my mother. He was my reason to fight for a better life. My son's birth was like a rebirth for me. The moment I saw him I wanted to live. I didn't want to go back to the miserable life I had before. I planned to keep moving forward. My son saved my life. He *was* my life.

"Notwithstanding she shall be saved in childbearing, if they continue in faith and charity and holiness with sobriety" (1 Timothy 2:15 KJV).

Returning to work left me emotional because I didn't want to leave my baby. I rushed home every day to snuggle with my little prince. I watched him sleep and reflected on all my bad decisions. I understood for the first time the heart of a mother. I realized how my mother must have felt discovering all that I'd done. She must have been plagued with hurt, confusion, anger and helplessness when she found out my struggles. I was determined to change. My life wasn't my main priority now with a son to protect, provide for and love with all of my being.

~Relapse~

All was well in our family for about 5 months after our son was born but then my husband showed signs of relapse. Glenn was living like a shadow in our home. He often moved through the house very quietly. When I walked into a room where he was sitting, he looked frightened. After repeatedly denying his relapse when asked, he finally admitted he was back on drugs and this time it was heroine. I stumbled upon his drug supplies in our home multiple times until one day I asked him to leave. He refused to leave, telling me he would give up drugs. History had repeated itself too often with his drug addiction, so I didn't believe he could quit alone. I wanted to separate from him and tried to lock him out. When I returned home from work I discovered that he'd broken into the house through a window. Discouraged, I continued with our daily routine as if nothing happened. I worked long, irregular hours while my mother cared for my son. Glenn returned from work before I did and picked up our son. I habitually called when I knew he would be home to check up on the baby. I rushed home after work just to alleviate the stress and worry about my son's safety.

A year passed and Glenn started to disappear for days at a time. Now our son was walking and talking so he often asked for his daddy. It made me sad to see him look out of the window in expectation of his father's return. I ran out of excuses to tell my son why daddy wasn't home. On the rare occasion he was home I would call to check in and my little toddler would answer and tell me his daddy was sleeping. One night I called and a young girl answered the phone telling me she was a runaway and my husband left her with our son. I immediately left work and hailed a taxi to go home. I entered my home and my son ran to me so I could scoop him up. He buried his face in my neck peering at the young runaway with one eye. I looked at her and asked probing questions to find out how she came to stay in my home. She was a runaway tagging along with my husband and his friend as they went looking for drugs. He came home to pick up our son from my mother and asked the runaway to babysit while he went out to buy drugs. I allowed her to sleep in my home for the night and then dropped her at a bus station the next day. I would not allow myself and my baby to live in danger any longer. I took emergency vacation to figure out my escape. My husband didn't return;

however, because fortunately he had been arrested. I welcomed the time away from him. I spent the day with my son just enjoying his chatter and play. At night I played music and danced around the house. It was physically painful to dance due to my recent surgery. I looked at my scar and stretch marks in the mirror and cried. I would never be able to dance the way I used to.

One morning as I played music my son toddled into the room and began to dance. I watched him and choked back tears. He turned and stretched his arms upward and jumped to the melody of the song. I cried when he finished and he came to console his mommy. I held him tight and kissed his face with a smile. I always danced as he slept so I was in awe of what I witnessed. God allowed me to see the beauty of freedom through my son. He was happy and free to be himself. He could dance and sing and play without fear. I couldn't allow him to experience fear that would muffle his voice and paralyze him. I knew I needed to leave my husband in order to protect my son. I decided the only way to separate from him was to move back in with my mom again. I gave up the rental house and returned to my mother's home. My move was complete in one week and I vowed never to return. I spent 13 years abused by this man and I would not allow my baby to experience the same hurt.

"For in the time of trouble he shall hide me in his pavilion: in the secret of his tabernacle shall he hide me; he shall set me up upon a rock" (Psalm 27:5 KJV).

After my separation, I returned to church in search of peace and forgiveness. I remembered the peace I felt as a young girl when I first accepted Jesus. I'd made so many bad decisions since that time and guilt weighed heavy in my heart. I needed to know I was forgiven and hoped to set a path toward a better life. I had witnessed my mother's transformation when she returned to church, so I knew Jesus could fix me. Couldn't He?

Living in my mother's house with her boyfriend, Chris was uncomfortable for me. He started becoming more and more controlling and cruel. I didn't want to live in a violent, controlling environment anymore but I needed shelter. Whenever Chris would start a disagreement with me my mother would come to my defense but I didn't want to cause trouble for her again. I needed to move on my own and take care of my son. I wanted him to grow up in a peaceful environment. He asked many questions about his father. I tried to explain why we moved and his daddy didn't live with us, but at three years old, he was too young to understand. He wore sadness on his little face and I couldn't distract his thoughts about his father. He missed his dad so I asked my husband to take him for weekend visits. My son cried during visits with his dad. I comforted him on the phone but he seemed upset most of the time. He was confused and told me he wanted to come home. Where was home? We didn't have a home. A home is more than a place to live; it's where you feel peace, joy and safety. I was working to give my son a real home.

"For every house is built by someone, but God is the builder of everything" (Hebrews 3:4 NIV).

My mother taught me that God speaks to us through His word. I started my own personal Bible study to bring clarity to my cloudy life. Each page revealed truth as I read through the chapters. God answered so many questions about my experiences and how to live a life pleasing to Him. I wondered how he could love me, given my broken history. I gave up so many of my passions because of the turmoil in my life. Much of the suffering I experienced was a direct result of my naive attempt to create my own perfect world. When one of my plans failed I devised an alternative plan. All the while I lived enslaved in sin. I hid from people and only went out when I had to, like Gideon. Gideon was hiding under an oak threshing wheat when the angel of the Lord appeared to him. He hid from the Midianites who constantly plundered everything from the Israelites, leaving them impoverished. The angel of the Lord came when the Israelites cried out to the Lord in distress.

Similar to Gideon, I felt like I'd lost so much and I just wanted to preserve what little I had. I lost hope of ever becoming anything other than a single mother surviving paycheck to paycheck. I questioned God, wondering where He was when I was suffering. Why didn't He help me? Darkness was part of my life no matter how sunny the sky appeared. I felt shame, fear and guilt. I couldn't figure out who I was and where I would land after my ride. After so many years of rejection, I truly believed I was destined for and deserved a life of misery. Determined to protect my son from feeling like an outcast, I provided all I could to shield him from lack. He would always know he was loved.

> *"Have mercy on me, O God according to your unfailing love; according to your great compassion blot out my transgressions. Wash away all my iniquity and cleanse me from my sin" (Psalms 51:1-2 NIV).*

I prayed every day for provision only to be greeted with silence. I looked for immediate results but when I looked to the heavens, manna didn't fall from the clouds. My faith wavered from day to day, depending on my emotions and the day's events. Church gave me a boost of faith but could sometimes make me feel alienated. The church I attended as a youth went from a handful of followers to thousands in the decade I was away. The music was so beautiful it seemed to pass straight into my heart. I watched so many people around me raise their hands and sing to God. I awkwardly raised my hands to mimic the others around me. I sang the lyrics to the songs and something inside ached from the pit of my stomach to the base of my throat. I didn't understand the reason for the longing I felt welling up inside. My eyes filled with tears and soon ran down my face to drip from my chin.

A woman unexpectedly hugged me and began to pray. I don't remember what she said but my sobs became harder and deeper. I cried until my head hurt. What was wrong with me? An usher offered me tissues to dry my face and I sat to listen to Pastor speak. There I sat like the prodigal son returning home. My pastor looked like he hadn't aged a day since I left the church years ago. I wanted to run to him like a lost daughter and have him reassure me that all would be well for me and my son. I imagined his children were very happy to have a father like him. He loved God and He was a good man. Good men were non-existent in my life. Pastor spoke with wisdom and confidence, meeting the eyes of the congregation. I heard the occasional "Amen" and "Hallelujah" come from the people but I stayed silent. I didn't want to miss a single word.

At the end of the sermon Pastor asked if there was anyone who wanted to accept Jesus. My heart beat hard as I walked up to the altar. I repeated a salvation prayer and the pastor congratulated all who responded. He said we were "saved." I've heard this before, I thought. Perhaps I would get my salvation right this time.

We were invited to stay and speak with the pastor after service so I stayed. I wanted to ask what it meant to be saved, but when the time came I never asked. I was ashamed of my lack of knowledge. I returned home to read the Bible verses in my salvation pack. I continued to attend church to learn more about Jesus and salvation. Trials continued to plague my life but my perspective was slowly changing.

"Therefore he is able to save completely those who come to God through him, because he always lives to intercede for them" (Hebrews 7:25 NIV).

Chapter 5

~A Father's Love~

My parents were very hard-working individuals. Even in their brokenness they instilled in me the importance of hard work to support yourself and your children. As a dancer I worked for multiple companies and choreographers at the same time to take care of myself. In addition I worked part-time in retail to supplement my pay when I couldn't find work as an artist. When I left the professional world of dance I continued teaching dance and working in retail. Now that I was a single mom, I needed more stability so I worked hard to get promoted at my retail job so I could earn enough to be independent. In retail moving up was easy as long as you proved your competency. It wasn't much different than training to be your best in dance technique to land the best roles in companies. After two years, I was offered a managerial position with benefits and good pay that would help me afford a small apartment of my own. My spirits were lifted and I decided to go out and celebrate. One of my co-workers invited me to free salsa classes. Excitement filled my heart at the thought of dancing again. I accepted the invitation and shopped for shoes and a dress. When the evening finally came, one after another of my co-workers cancelled until all reneged with an excuse. I resigned myself to going alone, but I was still filled with anticipation of a wonderful evening.

The salsa classes took place in the middle of the week at a salsa club in Manhattan. I was thrilled to learn a new dance style. This time I danced for pleasure, not to escape or for work. The class was broken up into an individual session and a partnering session. For the individual session, our group learned the basics of salsa technique. The first session ended with a break before the partnering session. I sat and watched as all the participants rushed to speak with the instructor or chat with each other. Everyone wore smiles and their faces glowed. I stood up and walked to the ladies room and stopped to look at myself in the mirror. I washed my hands all the while still staring at my reflection. I stalled, waiting for the last lady to leave before I smiled at myself in the mirror. I decided to wear smiles more often. Hopefully my smiles would have a real connection to my heart. I could hear the instructors announcing the partner session was about to begin so I rushed out to join. Ladies lined up facing the men, who stood in another line and I ran to insert myself in the middle of the line. We were instructed to take the hands of the person facing us to match with a partner. We were also told we would switch partners every so often to mix novice and intermediate dancers.

The gentleman I paired with was much older with a sly smile and a lazy right eye. He annoyed me with his random chatter on topics I had no interest in. I tried to keep my attention on the instructor in hopes he would focus more on the dance instruction. The instructor soon called for a partner switch to my relief. Before handing me off, the older gentleman leaned close to me and told me he was going home and invited me to come. Repulsed, I politely declined with a tight smile. He handed me to another gentleman and shuffled out the door.

My second partner was a handsome gentleman with the warmest brown eyes. He introduced himself as Carlos and asked my name before leading me to the dance floor. He danced with skill and charmed me with his gentle smile. When the instructor called for a switch of partners, he held onto my hands and winked at me. My heart jumped in my chest, and I giggled. We danced until the late evening. My night with Carlos was amazing, but I needed to return home. He was nice enough to offer to drive me to my car. I accepted his kind offer. We walked to his car and he politely opened the door for me. I watched him rush around to the driver seat and jump in with excitement. He talked the entire time as he navigated his way with my direction to my car. When we arrived at my car I expected him to try and kiss me. I was ready to push him away but he only gave me a business card and a friendly peck like I was his sister. I stepped out of his car; he politely said goodnight. It was a perfect ending to a great night. I thought it would be nice to have a friend I could go dancing with sometimes. If we remained friends there would be no heartbreak. Just like stage partners, where there are no attachments; just dance for the performance and it's over.

I drove home and quietly entered the house. My son was sound asleep and I kissed his sweet face. I pulled out the business card to read it. The front listed Carlos' name, title and the location of his job. On the back was his home phone number. I noticed we worked on the same street. I figured I could meet him and we could ride to dance class together each week. I called him a few days later to plan the next salsa class, but his answering service picked up. Disappointed and embarrassed, I left a message in hopes he would return my call. Why did I feel so drawn to this man? I knew I couldn't get involved with anyone. Since my husband was released from jail he'd stalked me at work and my mother's home. I didn't know how to get away from him or if it was good for my son to be torn from his father. If my husband knew I was dancing with another man in a club he wouldn't care if it was innocent. He would react violently and people could get hurt. I had no clue what to do to prevent his erratic behavior. I only knew that I wouldn't return to the life I'd had with him.

*"Deliver me from mine enemies, O my God: defend me
from them that rise up against me" (Psalms 59:1 NIV).*

Carlos was kind and respectful like no other man I'd known. He intrigued me when we met, with his gentle nature and his clever conversation that made me smile until my face hurt. The day after I called Carlos, I was paged to the phone at work and I rushed to answer, concerned it was about my son. When I answered I heard Carlos' voice and I trembled with excitement. We planned to meet for lunch the next day since we worked a few avenues apart. I floated around work for the rest of the night.

The next day, I left after work to rendezvous with Carlos at a nearby diner. Our conversation was vibrant just like the first time I met him. He was intelligent, funny, and full of life. Whenever he looked at me I felt drawn in by the warmth and gentleness in his eyes. His smile was bright and cheerful. I didn't recall any man ever looking at me with such genuine kindness. I couldn't help but feel giddy around him. When our lunch date was over, I started to walk away, then turned back and gave Carlos a small peck and waved goodbye. He looked a bit stunned and I wondered if I'd moved too fast. I knew very little about him other than how kind he was.

For the remainder of my workday and on my commute home, regret and fear plagued my mind. What if I'd offended him? Why couldn't I think before acting? I rushed home and sat distracted by my thoughts when Carlos contacted me. My heart hammered in my chest and a cold chill ran through my body as we spoke. After a few minutes of unrelated chatter he mentioned my show of affection during lunch. To my relief he was flattered and expressed his interest in exploring a relationship with me. He did invite me out again. I felt my heartbeat slow down to a normal rate. In the past, death had tried to claim my life for so many years as trials drained my life. Just as rigor mortis waited to harden every part of me, a new burst of life revived my dying heart. I was alive with breath in my lungs and new hope for the future.

"I will give you a new heart and put a new spirit in you; I will remove from you your heart of stone and give you a heart of flesh" (Ezekiel 36:26 NIV).

As the weeks and months passed, I learned more and more about Carlos and realized he possessed the characteristics of the husband I prayed for as a teen. He was loving, kind, responsible, and handsome. He had a casual way of looking at me with his head tilted to the side smiling softly that told me he appreciated me. His compliments were plentiful and made me feel beautiful. He accepted my son and treated him kindly. I didn't feel worthy of such a great blessing. Occasionally feelings of guilt and shame resurfaced with memories of my damaged, soiled life. I was worthless in my eyes and afraid for Carlos to know my past. I trusted God that he was my knight in shining armor. I was falling in love with Carlos and told him so. He didn't respond the same but thanked me for telling him. It was humbling that he didn't reciprocate a statement of love but it was fine with me. I wouldn't stop loving him just because he didn't respond in kind. He was always in my thoughts. I waited for his calls every day and raced to spend time with him when I had the time. I'd lie on my bed at night and envision our life together. I hoped I could find my happy place with Carlos and that perhaps we could build a real home together some day.

On one of our many dates, Carlos told me if ever I met his mother I would know I was special to him. I'd forgotten that he told me this so when he presented an envelope containing an invitation to her home, I cried. He thought I was special enough to meet his mother! I didn't think much of myself but I wanted to be the best woman I could be for him. I needed to cleanse certain people and behaviors from my life. Maybe then I would feel worthy of such a wonderful man. Maybe then I would have peace.

I filed for divorce from my first husband. He contested the divorce and avoided contact with me so he wouldn't get served the legal papers. I filed again with the city and the court granted my divorce. I was finally free of legal ties to Glenn. He continued to stalk me and was verbally abusive whenever we made contact. I allowed Glenn visitation with our son, but he cancelled many of the visits or didn't show to pick up our son. I felt the hurt for my little son, waiting by the window for his father. He didn't deserve the hurt he continually experienced. I tried making excuses but I ran out of things to say. Glenn wasn't a responsible parent. I confronted him about his inconsistencies when he explained why he didn't show up for visits. He admitted to taking our son with him when he went to buy drugs a few times and realizing that it was wrong, he decided he didn't want him to suffer any harm. He requested to stop visitation and so I did. I saw that Glenn did love his son but was trapped in his addiction. He was allowed to call our son until his calls turned into small interrogations. During one such call I could hear my son cry in response to his father's questions on the phone. I took the phone and I could hear him yelling out insults toward me. I didn't want my son to be caught in the middle of our disagreements. I hung up the phone and disconnected it from the wall before consoling my son. I tried my best to explain why his daddy was angry and told him we would need to give him time to feel better. He wasn't contributing anything positive to our son's life, so I decided to take drastic measures to protect my son. I changed my phone number and arranged for a job transfer to different location. I had to eliminate all contact with my ex-husband and raise my son on my own. Protecting my little boy was my main focus. I wanted to close the door on my past and never look back.

Every Sunday in church I listened to the sermons hoping to find peace and cleansing for my soul. I dedicated my son in church and enrolled in Bible study. I continued to purge old habits and people from my past. Church became a hospital for me. There I found truth that healed my wounds. My guilt stemmed from my sins against God. I deserved death, according to Scripture, for all my sins. Yet here I stand in the land of the living where God continues to meet me and reveal His compassion.

"For I know my transgressions, and my sin is always before me. Against you, you only, have I sinned and done what is evil in your sight; so you are right in your verdict and justified when you judge. Surely I was sinful at birth, sinful from the time my mother conceived me. Yet you desired faithfulness even in the womb; you taught me wisdom in that secret place" (Psalms 51:3-6 NIV).

Our Pastor explained how Jesus died for all and I was washed clean when I repented and accepted Him. For the first time I grasped the meaning of salvation. The most beautiful part of all was I knew Carlos was saved. He would explain concepts from the Bible and quote Scripture relating to issues that we discussed. Carlos is a righteous man who is like the tree in Psalm 1:3 planted by streams of water. What set him apart from all the other men I'd known was his connection to God. He was sent by God to bring restoration after destruction. I was so grateful and prayed I would be a blessing to him as well.

Through all my cleansing and transformation somehow I fell into a deep darkness. I didn't understand why I felt such heaviness in my spirit. I had Christ in my life; a good job; a wonderful, godly man; a place to live; a healthy child and I had put my past behind me. Yet I couldn't forget the past. I knew God had forgiven me, but I couldn't forgive myself. I shared my concern with Carlos and he gave me a book to read and suggested prayer counseling with his pastor. The book helped me through the grief I'd experienced because of my terminated pregnancy. I wasn't sure how the prayer counseling could help me, but I was willing to try. My last counseling experience as a teen left me with a negative impression about counselors but perhaps pastoral counseling could help me. It was worth trying if I could get relief from my blue mood. I agreed to the prayer counseling at Carlos' church. It would be necessary to attend the church and meet the pastor before asking for counseling. I didn't know how to handle this. I didn't like change and I'd just recently returned to my church after a long absence. My church had grown exponentially over the years that I was away; it was so large I felt invisible. I'd been away so long that the few familiar faces that remained no longer remembered me. I didn't feel fully integrated yet, so I felt fearful to ask for help. Perhaps a new church was best. I started to attend church with Carlos.

Carlos attended a small storefront church in the South Bronx. The church members were loving and strong in their faith. Everyone welcomed me the minute I arrived. The pastor and his wife were so sweet and passionate about serving Christ. They quickly embraced me as their spiritual daughter. I felt at home immediately. God's love poured out to me through each member of the church. I found acceptance, this time not because I was a skillful dancer, but because I was a child of God.

"For ye are all sons of God through faith in Christ Jesus" *(Galatians 3:26 KJV).*

My first prayer counseling session is the only one I remember. The pastor asked me a few questions about my family history then explained all of the generational curses that were evident. He began to pray and I felt the spirit of God move all around me and stir within me. Pastor prayed for issues I knew I hadn't shared with him. He prayed about things that only God knew. My Father in heaven was speaking to me just like Jesus spoke to the woman at the well. I wept so much I thought I wouldn't have tears left in my body. The last words I remember hearing were "Give her a Father's love." I passed out. I felt darkness leave and light enter. I realized I needed to know my Father's love in order to be free. Flashbacks of all the times I'd felt alone and the times I almost died raced through my mind. The images that rushed through my mind weren't just memories. God was showing me all the times I was angry with Him because I thought He'd forgotten about me. Jesus was with me each time, wiping tears, protecting me, providing for me, and listening to me. I was never alone. My Savior never left my side. Despite my flaws Jesus truly loved me. Salvation didn't mean freedom from trials. That was my own selfish belief. Jesus suffered and died as payment for my sins even before I was born. He died so I could live and come to know Him. By faith I was saved. Everything was clear now. A Father's love isn't something to be earned; it's free and undeserved.

"But now that you have been set free from sin and have become slaves of God, the benefit you reap leads to holiness, and the result is eternal life. For the wages of sin is death, but the gift of God is eternal life in Christ Jesus our Lord" (Romans 6:22-23 NIV).

~And One Will Be Many~

With a new understanding of salvation, I started to think about my family going to heaven. I wanted them to know the joy of salvation. The thought of salvation for my family brought my great grandmother Rosalee to mind. I remembered she always carried a small Bible in the pocket of her housedress and muttered prayers all day. I then realized she was our prayer warrior and a deep well of wisdom from which I could drink. She was living in the South with her daughter when news of her hospitalization came to my mother. When my mother shared the news I had an uncontrollable pull in my spirit telling me that I needed to travel and see her. Somehow I knew she would be going home to be with the Lord soon and I wanted to be with her and ask her about her faith. I remember my entire life she was always present with a Bible in hand, praying for her family. As a child I chuckled along with my cousins at Grandma having her Jesus moments. I had no idea of the importance of her prayers over us.

My mother and I planned a road trip and drove to see Grandma with little Glenn. When we arrived I walked into Grandma's room to find her with an oxygen tank and facemask, looking sick. When she saw me she sat up and smiled as she removed her facemask. I introduced her to my son and he walked to her. She smiled and kissed him while he rambled questions about all the medical equipment in her room. When my son ran out to play, I hugged my grandmother and told her I was saved. She rejoiced in her frail voice and I took her hands, taking a mental picture of her to remember every detail etched in her appearance. I knew she was once a dancer and had worked as a nurse. Many people were healed through the very hands I held. Many babies were cradled in her arms including 17 of her own. I asked her about a ring she still wore and she said it was from her husband who had passed long ago. Then I asked how she came to know Jesus and she said, "Child, He knew me first."

"We love because he first loved us" (1 John 4:19 NIV).

I treasured her words and the time I spent with her before we returned home.

Two months later we received a call that Grandma had told her daughter and grandchildren she was going home to see Jesus and then took her last breath. My mother and I traveled south once again, this time for her home-going service. I looked at my grandmother's face, no longer alive but looking peaceful. I didn't expect to feel the pain of loss so deeply when I realized she would no longer be a phone call away. The pastor shared facts about my grandmother I never knew. She had accepted Jesus at barely 20 years old and served their church for 77 years. I wailed audibly and quickly walked away from her casket, only to be stopped by a relative who consoled me. I asked, "Who will pray for us now?" I went to my mother's car as we prepared to travel to the burial site. We drove over steep hills on the road and at the top of each incline I could see at least 30 cars ahead of us with police escorts. I looked to my right and saw construction workers and passersby with helmets, hats or hands over their hearts. Did they know my grandma? The procession was so grand and the honor paid to her by strangers was shocking. I felt sick to see her casket lowered into the dark, cold earth and stayed far from the activity. I continued to ask, "Who will pray for us now?" The Lord answered, "Where there was one, there will be many." With His promise I knew I would serve the Lord all of my days. My prayers would be for my family and friends to know the joy of salvation.

"But if serving the LORD seems undesirable to you, then choose for yourselves this day whom you will serve,

whether the gods your ancestors served beyond the Euphrates, or the gods of the Amorites, in whose land you are living. But as for me and my household, we will serve the LORD" (Joshua 24:15 NIV).

Chapter 6

~Dance for the Lord~

I continued to attend Carlos' church. Living with my mom had become uncomfortable with Chris living there. He was confrontational about everything but especially his belief that I should contribute more to the household. I agreed with his complaint but the daily confrontations affected me emotionally. I really couldn't tolerate the arguments and fights. After so many years of abuse I just wanted peace. He called me terrible names and I was disgusted with his tantrums. After one of our disputes I left with my son in my car, crying. I didn't know what to do anymore. I called my pastor for prayer. He listened calmly and advised me to leave, but I didn't have enough money to move. Carlos called and invited me to come and pray about moving. We prayed, then opened the local ads to look for apartments. I tried to tell him I didn't have money, but he hushed me and continued to look through the apartment ads. The first one we called was available to look at the same evening. I went to meet the landlord and view the tiny apartment. It was small, but it would be a suitable home for me and my son.

I filled out all the paperwork for the apartment and left feeling doubtful. I didn't have the down payment or references to get approved. A few days later the landlord called to tell me to come sign the lease if I was still interested in the apartment. I was thrilled but still full of fear since I didn't have enough money to pay the rent and the security deposit. I called Carlos to tell him the news and he said he would accompany me to sign the lease. I met Carlos and tried to tell him again that I couldn't afford to pay the landlord, but he encouraged me to move forward. Carlos took the paperwork to verify that everything was in order and gave me the lease to sign. I read and signed with my hands shaking, holding back tears. I handed the papers back to Carlos who then gave them to the landlord with a rent and security deposit check for me. I was speechless as he turned to look at me with a knowing look in his eyes. He reminded me that God provides. I didn't deserve this wonderful man and yet God placed him in my life.

I invited the women from the church to come to my home and celebrate my new beginning. We all sang and danced praises to the Lord. I finally had a home. It would be a place where I could feel safe and find peace. I felt I could give my son a better life there.

"Therefore do not be anxious, saying, 'What shall we eat?' or 'What shall we drink?' or 'What shall we wear?' For the Gentiles seek after all these things, and your heavenly Father knows that you need them all" (Matthew 6:31-32 NIV).

I became a regular attendee at Carlos' church. I volunteered to teach the children and I attended group studies mid-week. My son attended the children's church and made friends with the other children. This was a place where I felt accepted and was able to learn and grow. I had experiences in our church like I never had before. There was something different inside of me. I loved God more than I could express and often cried during worship. One Sunday I lifted my hands during worship as I sang and rejoiced, when the pastor pulled me out in front of the congregation and said, "Dance for the Lord!" I was stunned and my heart raced with fear. What did he mean? I dropped to my knees and wept. Why couldn't I dance? The pastor would try this again with the same response from me. I didn't know what he expected me to do. How do you dance for the Lord? I trained for years to be excellent in my craft, but my body shut down each time Pastor called me out. There was a time when I could dance for hours to nothing but the music in my head or to the sound of the ocean, but I felt so inadequate when asked to dance in church. How could I break free of this paralyzing fear?

"I will instruct you and teach you in the way you should go; I will counsel you with my loving eye on you" (Psalms 32:8 NIV).

~Dance with Me~

Months later during worship, an unfamiliar song called "Dance with Me" began to play. I closed my eyes and listened to the words. My spirit jumped and I felt warm and weightless. With my eyes still closed I saw the Lord looking at me and felt Him take my hands to spin me around and around. My feet no longer touched the floor. The Lord held me in His arms and danced with me. I felt myself float as the Lord took the lead in our dance. As quickly as it began it ended and I opened my eyes and looked up at the people singing. I realized I was no longer standing. I was looking up from the floor with displaced chairs around me. Everything sounded muffled as I sat up. I felt hands lift me and sit me in a chair to recover. Worship continued as if nothing happened. How did I get on the floor? Did the Lord drop me? I asked Pastor what happened and he explained the manifest presence of the Holy Spirit. I couldn't believe it! God came to dance with me!

"The LORD your God is with you, the Mighty Warrior who saves. He will take great delight in you; in his love he will no longer rebuke you, but will rejoice over you with singing" (Zephaniah 3:17 NIV).

I started teaching dance to the children in church but never danced myself. I didn't know what dancing for the Lord would look like so rather than make a fool of myself, I stayed in my seat. I started to see movement in my mind during worship songs. It had been so long since I could hear a song and see dance. My son never saw me dance but started dancing to a slow song that played on the radio. It was so beautiful to see he had the passion to dance. I reminisced about the first time I saw him dance as a baby. He continued to amaze me.

"See! The winter is past; the rains are over and gone. Flowers appear on the earth; the season of singing has come, the cooing of doves is heard in our land" (Song of Solomon 2:11-12 NIV).

~The Two Become One~

Two years passed and Carlos and I were considered by the church the next candidates for marriage. He was a tremendous blessing to my son and me. He stood by me through every trial and became a father figure for my son. It was a welcome change to feel loved by him. People buzzed around us asking when we would marry. I'd look at Carlos for a response and he would say, "In time." I avoided giving an answer. Instead with a smile, I shrugged and giggled. I was happy to have him in my life, but deep inside I desired more. During one of our group Bible studies, a sister in Christ prophesized that I would marry a pastor. I politely smiled, then just ignored her. Carlos wasn't a pastor and he was the one I wanted to marry.

Two years turned to three and Carlos still hadn't asked me to marry him. I figured I'd better look within to see if I was a suitable wife for this wonderful man. I started to cleanse and purge habits and people to prepare myself for the moment he would ask for my hand. I wondered how and where he would propose. Every special occasion I styled my hair and dressed special in anticipation of a proposal. Each time the evening would end with a good night. I was losing hope that he would ask me to be his wife.

Carlos started to search for a house to purchase and asked if I would come to look at prospective homes with him. I agreed and we looked at a few homes until Carlos purchased one. His new home was a two-family dwelling with three bedrooms in the upper dwelling. He moved into his new home and also moved his mom into the first floor dwelling. I remained in my tiny apartment with my son still awaiting a marriage proposal. I was happy for him, but it was hard to remain patient. I settled back into my routine of work and caring for my son. Carlos helped me care for my little boy when I worked late. He picked up little Glenn from school and waited for me to pick him up after work at his home. After an especially long day I arrived at Carlos' home to pick up my son. He invited me to the kitchen and told me he loved me. I was worn out from work and barely gave him a chance to speak. He poured out his heart and bent on one knee to propose. I said yes and he presented me with a diamond ring. This would be the first marriage proposal I ever experienced and the most beautiful diamond I had ever seen. He thought enough of me to prepare a place for me by purchasing a home. He valued me enough to invest in a diamond ring. I couldn't wait to marry him. I wanted to shout from the tallest skyscraper. He wanted to marry me because he loved me. He thought I was worthy.

I was excited about planning a wedding. I didn't have a wedding with my first husband so I had no idea what to do first. Thankfully the sisters at church along with my childhood friend, Pamela and close cousin, Charrisse helped with all my plans. For months I planned, the location, music, flowers, food, dresses, guest lists and more. I was overwhelmed with every detail but joyful. I would become one with the man I'd prayed for 15 years ago. Carlos was the man God kept just for me. At just the right time, the Lord ordained our meeting and now we were preparing to join our lives until death. I didn't grow up with an example of a good marriage, but I knew it was possible for marriage to be filled with love and joy with God in the center.

A few months before our wedding, Carlos and I took premarital classes to prepare to enter into covenant. Upon completion of the premarital classes, our pastor unexpectedly announced he would be leaving and Carlos would be ordained as the pastor of our church. I recalled the prophecy the sister shared two years prior. This was confirmation that God orchestrated our union. I was truly in awe of how fast circumstances were unfolding. I would be married in two months and take on the title of a pastor's wife. How could I live up to the demands of the position and still be a good wife and mother? I would have to talk with people and care for them. I would need to support my husband in ministry. I didn't know anything about ministry. I didn't know how to be a wife either. I kept my focus on my wedding plans. All other plans we would deal with as they came.

On our wedding day I was so nervous I fainted in the beauty parlor. I was physically ill before leaving. Why was this happening? I loved Carlos and I couldn't wait for this day. I returned home with a host of bridesmaids fussing over me. The fainting spell had all of them concerned I wouldn't be well for the ceremony. I assured them I wouldn't miss my wedding. I slipped into my dress, applied my makeup and put on my jewelry. The photographer came in to capture memorable moments like my dad fixing my shoe, my mom placing my veil on my head and my close cousin fixing my tiara. I looked in the mirror and smiled. I looked like a princess. This day I wore the most beautiful dress I had ever owned and it was just for one day. This one day marked the beginning of my new life with Carlos. I carefully stepped down the stairs and peered out at the day. The sky darkened with clouds and rain poured. My father came to the rescue with a large umbrella to escort every bridesmaid to the limo he rented for me. Carlos' mother emerged looking elegant and smiled at me and she handed me a wedding gift. I looked at it and blushed when I saw it was a negligée. She leaned in and said, "Give me grandchildren." I giggled and stuffed her gift in my bag.

My father returned for me completely soaked. He was dressed so handsome and stood in the rain holding an umbrella over me to keep me dry. My daddy loved me. For all the years he missed in my life, this moment meant so much to me. I stepped into the limo to a checklist recited by my maid of honor, Pamela. I loved her so much. We'd remained friends since the age of 13. Twenty years of friendship and we were still close. Charrisse smiled and hugged me. She was like a sister to me my entire life. She was present through the dark times when I separated from my first husband. God surrounded me with people to help me through my troubles. They kept me hopeful in my trials.

The limo pulled up to the church and my father jumped out to open the door. I rushed in the church with all my bridesmaids checking my appearance. They all looked at me with tears and smiles. I blinked away my tears and looked toward the door where my father waited to give me away. My son walked out as the ring bearer with my niece as the flower girl. They were dressed as mini versions of Carlos and myself. Pamela's daughter and my young cousin walked out together looking so small but with a purposeful stride. Each of my bridesmaids marched and I was left waiting for my music.

My music started and my father held out his arm for me to hold. I stepped out to see all of my guests standing with smiles and tears. My mother stood in front looking proud and emotional. When I looked at my future husband, I choked back tears. He looked at me with tears filling his warm brown eyes. I would look into those eyes every day for the rest of my life. In this moment I was Cinderella being rescued by Prince Charming and beginning our happily ever after. Our wedding was like a fairy tale come true. We both wrote our own vows and read them to each other. I poured everything into my vows for Carlos and when I heard his vows, something inside me relaxed, knowing he would protect and love me for the rest of our days. After our tearful exchange, our pastor announced Carlos had a vow for my little boy. I had no idea he'd prepared something for little Glenn. Carlos bent down on one knee and held Glenn's little hands as he whispered a vow to him. He hugged him and stood up to everyone's applause and tears. I looked at him with tears in my eyes as the pastor pronounced us a family and all three of us marched down the aisle.

"For this reason a man will leave his father and mother and be united to his wife, and the two will become one flesh" (Ephesians 5:31 NIV).

A Family Ministry

A few months after our wedding, our pastor moved to Florida and appointed Carlos pastor of our church. I chose to put thoughts of the increased responsibility of managing a church on delay until after our wedding. Now here I was faced with the challenge, without counsel. We were newlyweds with plans to have more children and I was back in college. What was it like to be the wife of a pastor? Would people look to me for prayer and counsel? I wasn't qualified for the position of "first lady." I lacked wisdom and maturity.

"If any of you lacks wisdom, you should ask God, who gives generously to all, without finding fault, and it will be given to you" (James 1:5 NIV).

There were adjustments in my life that were necessary as a new wife. I spent the majority of my day at work leaving little time for anything else. I had a routine work schedule of more than 40 hours per week and travel was additional time to account for. I enrolled my son in school as soon as he was old enough so that I could work to support him. My son spent more quality time with teachers in school than with me. Teachers were poor substitutes for the love and affirmation a child needs from his parents. As a single mom, I was away from my child 12-16 hours a day. It hurt me to look into my son's eyes as I kissed him goodbye and rushed to work. Now that I had additional assignments, I worried I would see him less. My son started to have difficulty in school and Carlos suggested I homeschool to spend more time with little Glenn and reassure him. Carlos worked full time to support our family and I cut my hours at work in half. I homeschooled little Glenn and went to school part time to earn my Bachelors of Science degree.

He spoke to my heart when he suggested it was a perfect adjustment since we were planning to have more children. I thought I would feel inferior or be viewed as lazy and insignificant if I were a stay-at-home mom. All my fears were washed away with Carlos' words of affirmation. He looked at me and told me he valued all I could do to maintain our home and raise our children. He reminded me each day of how much he appreciated me. Each night when he settled in to sleep, he whispered sweet words to remind me of his love. In the morning he sang cheerfully to greet the day. Walls that were built to guard my heart were shaken down by the love Carlos showered on me. I was eager to serve him as the wife he deserved. I willingly submitted to him because of his goodness and sacrifice for our family.

I watched Carlos work a full day at work, then come home to prepare for Sunday service. Sometimes I helped him prepare worship songs for service and also taught children's church on Sundays. In summer, I taught Vacation Bible School to children in our church and neighborhood. We settled into a steady flow of work, school and ministry. Being in leadership wasn't easy but the Lord always gave us what we needed to care for His people.

The Lord blessed us with our daughter, Denivia in 2005. Again I had a difficult pregnancy and I delivered prematurely by C-section. Carlos was in the room when she was delivered. She gave a tiny bird-like cry that entered my heart. The doctors let me see her briefly before taking her away. She was so small… like a little doll. I was overjoyed that I'd been given a daughter to love and train up. I had a dream before she was born and in my dream I could see her so clearly. She had her father's warm brown eyes, curly cherry brown hair and my bronze complexion. My princess looked exactly like I dreamed she would. When we arrived home I introduced little Glenn to his baby sister. He looked nervous but intrigued by her tiny frame. Now I had my boy and my girl. I started decorating Denivia's room. I would make her room mystical and feminine just as I would have if it were my room. Her walls were my favorite shade of purple for royalty and covered with butterflies. Butterflies were my favorite animal. As a young girl my mother gave me a butterfly net to catch them. I remember running and scooping them up with my little net as my mother warned me not to crush them. She told me their wings were like butter and could melt if you held them. I loved to watch them flutter through the grass and flowers. They represented freedom and transformation. Butterflies went through a period of darkness before they could fly. I thought my life was like the life of a butterfly. Once I was bound, now I was free. My daughter would be free.

As soon as my princess could walk, she danced in front of the church to everyone's delight. She filled my heart with joy as she jumped and spun around to the music with freedom. I didn't know the kind of complete freedom my daughter displayed. As I watched her dance to the music I yearned to break free and dance with her. She was my free spirit.

"It is for freedom that Christ has set us free. Stand firm, then, and do not let yourselves be burdened again by a yoke of slavery" (Galatians 5:1 NIV).

When my daughter was two years old, I became pregnant again. I was so sick and weak all the time and my doctor informed me that once again I was a high-risk case. I worried about my baby and prayed for good health. She told me there was a slight chance I would need a hysterectomy if I began to hemorrhage during delivery. After our conversation I believed I would die in childbirth. I had tremendous peace about dying but I worried about my children and husband. I prayed that if the Lord decided to take me He would take care of them for me. I was admitted into the hospital at seven months pregnant. My doctor kept me for 20 days. During that time I mourned my family, sure I would not return home. On the 20th day my husband was called in for

63

the delivery of our little boy. As I lay on the table, Carlos stayed with me, standing firm at my left side. His face was comforting as the doctors worked on me. I heard my son cry and saw him as the nurse brought him to me, then I passed out. In the darkness of my mind, I kissed my newborn son and saw him reach for me. I wanted to live to raise my little boy. I saw the faces of my children and husband flash in my mind. Then I saw my parents. Everyone was sad and sadness washed over me. I'd overcome so much and I didn't want to leave everyone sad. I felt it should have been a celebration of new life.

Our miracle baby boy, Ayden Joshua, was born in 2008. He was delivered prematurely by C-section. He was so frail when he was born at 5 lbs. 1 oz. He had trouble breathing and eating. When I was somewhat recovered from surgery, I slowly walked to the Neonatal Intensive Care Unit (NICU). I braced myself with one hand on the wall and the other holding my midsection, doubled over in pain. This was nothing new for me. I'd done this with my previous children, but there was more of an urgency with my youngest. I was drawn to him, knowing my presence would make a difference in his progress. I spent time with him, talking, touching and feeding him. I knew he would live. In a few months he grew big and strong. Watching his growth reminded me of all the times I'd felt helpless and weak. God was my strength to press through. Ayden has natural goodness that amazes me for such a young child. He served as my strength.

"God is our refuge and strength, a very present help in trouble" (Psalms 46:1 NIV).

Chapter 7

~Restored Passion~

A few months after our youngest was born, my husband decided that we would move the church to a location closer to our home. We were sharing space with another church and we hadn't seen growth in the church in five years. We couldn't find a suitable space so we started holding service in our home.

Our pastor returned from Florida and told us to try attending a church nearby. He told us Harvest Fields Community Church had ministries for the entire family. We started by sending Glenn, who was thirteen at the time, to youth ministry. He loved the youth services and made friends with many of the other teens. We followed a month later and loved it as well. It was nice to sit with my husband and receive the word of God. We were due for a rest period after 5 years of ministry. Our family needed spiritual growth. Our existing congregation followed us to the church as well. Our new church welcomed our family with open arms. My husband was reunited with friends he knew in his former church and I made new friends within the congregation.

Two months later there was a series of announcements made about dance ministry sign ups. I wasn't sure I could dance anymore with all the surgeries and I was still carrying pregnancy weight, but I signed up. I was so excited and attended every rehearsal. We ministered right before Christmas. This was my first time dancing for the Lord. Our pastor who had pulled me out to dance in the past, told my husband this was what he was trying to get me to do years ago, dance for the Father. I felt comforted that I ministered with a group. I didn't feel ready to dance alone.

A month later the choreographer wanted to minister the same dance again. I felt we needed something fresh and new. I was in my last year of college, so I made school my priority and dropped out of dance ministry. I hoped the next time we danced it would be a new choreography and a little more advanced. Two months later, I returned to rehearsal and was told that we would minister the same piece yet a third time. There was something inside of me that wanted growth and I knew I couldn't continue to repeat the same dance. I tried to ask the leader if I could choreograph something but I didn't have the chance to do so before I decided to completely remove myself from the ministry. I was new to dance ministry, but I didn't fit into this particular system. When we go to church we sing different songs each week that relate to the message. Shouldn't we as dancers have a fresh choreography that relates to the sermon as well? The first time we danced it was great, the second time people would wonder why we were dancing the same piece. I felt people would turn their attention away if they were seeing the same dance the third time. Perhaps I was only concerned about my own reputation, but I didn't want wrong perceptions about something I'd been passionate about my entire life.

"Neither do people pour new wine into old wineskins. If they do, the skins will burst; the wine will run out and the wineskins will be ruined. No, they pour new wine into new wineskins, and both are preserved" (Matthew 9:17 NIV).

One of my dear sisters in Christ died that year. She was a faithful servant and wonderful mentor. She trusted God for everything and gave so much of herself to help others. My husband was due to speak at her funeral and I helped him gather information for the obituary from her daughter. I returned home exhausted and as I retired to my bed, my husband told me I should speak at our sister's funeral. On the verge of sleep I muttered that I would dance for her. It was as if someone else said it and a surge of fear filled me and jolted me awake. Could I dance for the Lord alone?

The Lord would answer me by sending His ministers to dance at our church. I sat in the sanctuary as our pastor announced a special presentation by dancers. The ministers danced in with arms opening from ballet 5th position adorned in white and gold. I watched them twirl, leap and battement with skill and joy for the Lord. I felt my heart beat so hard I thought my chest would burst. I stood up mesmerized by the beauty of every dancer. I felt a pull in my spirit. I wanted to dance with the same joy they expressed. There was something in the atmosphere that I couldn't describe in my own words. The dancers changed the atmosphere. I went to meet them after service. I needed to find out whom they were and how to find them. I met the director's wife and she graciously gave me the information I needed to contact the ministry. The group name was Dance Ministry Institute and I discovered they conducted classes that I could attend. Every dancer wore a glow of confidence that made me feel at home. I made my decision to dance for the funeral.

> "Let them praise his name with dancing and make music
> to him with timbrel and harp" (Psalms 149:3 NIV).

The closer the date for the funeral, the more nervous I became. I was so busy caring for my home, completing my bachelor's degree and helping with details for the funeral that I never had the opportunity to choreograph a dance. The day of the funeral I went to a private area behind the viewing area and prayed for the Holy Spirit to take over. I was shaking and my heartbeat vibrated through my entire body. I prayed that I would not shut down like I'd done before. What would I feel when I danced? Would the Lord meet me like before? The music started and everything around me faded. I felt warm and calm as I danced for my Father. The steps came easy as if I'd never stopped dancing. All of the years I trained and worked were not lost. When I finished I returned to the private area and thanked God for His presence. Dancing for my heavenly Father restored the passion I lost years ago dancing in the world.

I sought out and joined the dance ministry that visited our church. Dance Ministry Institute, simply known as DMI consisted of dancers from different churches that came together to minister the Gospel through dance. The director, Robert Evans and his wife, Selena were most welcoming when I joined the ministry. It was wonderful to be surrounded by dancers who were also believers. I asked so many questions about dance in the church and one of the students gave me a book to read, Dance! (God's Holy Purpose) by Ann Stevenson.

Dr. Ann Stevenson is one of many pioneers that set out to teach God's holy purpose for dance. In her book she explains how the enemy took the art of dance and distorted it into a perverted version of God's original holy purpose. She said that the arts are now being restored to glorify God. I soon came away with a better understanding of why I'd lost interest in dancing for the world. I didn't have a clear purpose back then. I was looking for an escape and I needed to be set free. I needed to find who I was in Christ, then dancing would connect me to Him. There was much to learn and I wanted to meet with the dance pioneers and sit under their mentorship.

DMI called for volunteers to dance in a special presentation for Good Friday at my church and I volunteered. It was wonderful ministering with this group. My daughter and older son ministered as well. The dancers became like family after a short time. In the past when I danced with professional companies, many of the dancers were envious and competitive. I understood that the purpose for the worldly dance and dancing for the Lord were different and would attract different people. This was my season of discovery of my purpose for Christ.

~His Plan, Not Our Plan~

After six years, the day had finally come for me to graduate college. My parents, husband and children would all attend the ceremony. I arrived early with my family and prepared to receive my degree—long overdue. I left college in my twenties because I couldn't afford to pay tuition. My husband encouraged me to finish after we married and now I would do what I'd set out to do 15 years prior. I graduated with a Bachelor of Science in biology from a four-year institution. It took me six years to finish since I took time off when I gave birth to my youngest children. There were problems in a few of my classes since they challenged my faith at times. My faith in God never faltered but became stronger with each new challenge. I ministered to two of my professors who had questions about God. I always believed science was an enemy of faith in God, but that is far from the truth. I found that science strengthened my faith in God because of all that I learned.

I sat and waited for my name to be called to receive my diploma. I walked across the stage to the cheers and whistles of my family, honored by their compliments. We all climbed in our cars to celebrate over lunch and as we drove to my favorite restaurant I read the many cards from my family. I saved my mother's card for last. In her neat handwriting she simply stated, "And the poem has not ended, my hand is still here for you to hold." I laid my head back in the car with closed eyes as tears rolled down my face. My husband and children looked confused and concerned, but I couldn't speak so I smiled holding the card up. I was 11 years old when she wrote my first graduation poem. My heart overflowed with gratitude and joy that my mother remembered 27 years later her promise to me. She was always available when I was in need and continued to be a tremendous support. As we exited our cars I reached for her and hugged her tight, inhaling her perfume just like I used to when I was a little girl. She smiled wide as I thanked her and we both giggled before joining the rest of my family for lunch. God ordained this beautiful woman, my mother, to remind me God will never forget me.

"See, I have engraved you on the palms of my hands; your walls are ever before me" (Isaiah 49:16 NIV).

I had plans to apply to graduate school to work towards becoming a physical therapist and continue to study as a dance minister. I applied to several physical therapy programs. It took several weeks for the first school to respond. I felt my heart race as I opened the digital message. When I read the words on the screen my heart dropped. It was a rejection. Week after week I received rejections from every physical therapy school I applied to. I felt lost and unsure of my future. Perhaps this was not the purpose God had for me. I needed to make a decision on what career I would pursue. I would work towards becoming a biology teacher or nurse. It was a hard decision because each had positive and negative aspects to the position. Nurses work long hours but the pay is good and I enjoy serving people. Teachers have long prep times and paperwork but have summers off. What was my purpose?

Chapter 8

~*Dancing for Him*~

I began to search the Internet for more resources and found Dancing for Him Ministries. Pastor Lynn Hayden the founder and dance pioneer for Christ held dance conferences, but they were too far south and I couldn't travel so far with young children. I found one Dancing for Him Conference that would be in Virginia, which was only an 8-hour drive for me. I was so excited and asked my husband if I could go. He agreed and I registered for the conference. About a week later my husband lost his job but he insisted I still go on the trip to the conference. I set out driving early in the morning with my daughter and we arrived 10 hours later at our hotel. I could barely sleep in anticipation of what I would experience and learn at the conference.

I arrived at the conference with my daughter the next morning and signed in. When I stepped into the doorway I froze when I saw all the dancers worshipping freely with flags and long pieces of fabric called billows. One man stood towering above everyone, waving the only white flag in the room. I felt someone take my hand and saw it was Pastor Lynn Hayden. She spoke in a gentle voice and led me to a group of dancers. She told me to mirror the movement of the leader. My daughter joined in as well. I felt myself getting lost in the intimacy of dancing with my Father. Pastor Lynn prophetically danced for us as we watched. She spoke to me and told me she saw a passionate fire all around me. How did she know that? This was God speaking through her to me. I cried so much because I felt pieces of my life connecting. Everything that I lived through was allowed in order for me to come to the Lord. He led me here to show me a Father's love once more.

"You make known to me the path of life; you will fill me with joy in your presence, with eternal pleasures at your right hand" (Psalms 16:11 NIV).

I went home full of zeal to dance for the Lord and tried to start a dance group, but it fell apart before it started. I was brokenhearted but I prayed and the Lord led me to bring Pastor Lynn Hayden to New York. I asked my pastor if I could host a conference at our church and he agreed. I didn't know what to expect but I felt like this would be big. The name of our conference was "Passionate" just like the word spoken to me. I was in awe of how God connected everything.

A few months later my husband returned to work and I was able to take dance classes to work on my technique. I ministered with my daughter in DMI's production of Nativity for Christmas. The experience was exhilarating and spiritually filling. I invited everyone that I thought could come. Many of our church members came as well. One of my family members accepted Christ immediately following the production. I saw firsthand that dance could minister the truth of the gospel and lead to salvation.

"Those who observe the dance are often as much participants as those who are dancing. Although they are not physically moving, the dance communicates feelings and experiences that make them feel included in the devotional act. Observers discover their worship is heightened to a point where their hearts become softened toward God."

Murray Silberling

Chapter 9

~Behold I do a New Thing~

I started the year 2012 on a high note after the Nativity production. I was looking forward to the upcoming NY conference and what would follow. God was moving fast. Our church was in the middle of a corporate fast and God gave me two Scriptures and a song.

> "Have I not commanded you? Be strong and courageous. Do not be afraid; do not be discouraged, for the Lord your God will be with you wherever you go" (Joshua 1:9 NIV).

> "Forget the former things; do not dwell on the past. See, I am doing a new thing! Now it springs up; do you not perceive it? I am making a way in the wilderness and streams in the wasteland" (Isaiah 43:18-19 NIV).

The song titled "Moving Forward" inspired me to choreograph a solo signifying my journey to move ahead in my walk with God. The choreography came quickly and I practiced for weeks. A week before I ministered the dance my family received bad news. My husband shared that our house was in foreclosure and we had a letter from the IRS saying we owed $30K in taxes. Because my husband was unemployed our mortgage payments fell behind and the mortgage company filed to foreclose. Our tax preparer had filed our taxes incorrectly for three years unbeknownst to us and we needed to pay it all back. My husband also lost his job again so we had limited resources to utilize. Now the Scriptures God gave me made sense. The Scriptures given to us were to prepare us. We needed to remain courageous and remember God is always with us. We also had to be aware of the new things God would do. I danced the following week with a new passion. I knew God would be with us and we would move forward with Him.

We had a wonderful turnout for the dance conference. We had nearly 90 participants and Pastor Lynn sold out of her resource products. I had a wonderful time getting to know Pastor Lynn and some of her students. With the few resources we had, my husband and I financed the conference. The most amazing part is that Pastor Lynn took an offering for us, and the amount was exactly what we spent on the conference. How wonderful and faithful God is. I really wanted to join the Dancing for Him School and I expressed my desire to my husband. I didn't expect him to pull from our savings to pay for my school but he said we would make it happen and we did. Pastor Lynn helped me get all the resources I needed for a discount and I registered for school.

Chapter 10

~Jubilee Dance~

During my first year of school, I taught a summer class, started a small dance group and my company *Jubilee Dance Studio Inc.* (restoration, celebration, freedom). The name of my company comes from the Year of Jubilee described in the book of Leviticus, the 25th chapter. In the year of Jubilee all property was restored to people and slaves were freed in the 50th year. I imagined the celebrations during this time of restoration. I saw God restoring dance to the church and I wanted to join His work. My small dance group was made up of dancers with little dance training but they each had a heart for God that was so strong, when they worshiped, they moved people. I loved each of them dearly and watched them grow as dance ministers. We all worked to learn, pray and minister together. We ministered to people and to each other. I read a quote in one of the books assigned in school that changed my view of dancers in the church.

> *"I have heard it said that it is easier to teach a minister*
> *to dance than it is to teach a dancer to minister."*
> *Lynn Hayden*

In 2013, I graduated my first year of Dancing for Him school. I wanted to continue into the second year, but my husband and I didn't have the funds. God really sustained us the last few years and I was grateful that we still had a home and enough food to eat.

One day I received a message from Pastor Lynn offering a scholarship for her second year course and I joyfully accepted. I couldn't wait to study a second year with Pastor Lynn.

As I started the second year of school I also started teaching dance technique to dance ministers in various churches. There was a hunger and a need for the dancers to learn more formal training.

> *"Taking some formal training might help to expand your dance repertoire. If you know only ten moves, then you have only ten moves with which to express all that God pours into you! The more you know, the more you can use and the more you can offer for God to anoint!"*
> Heather Clark

The creative director of our church approached me to tell me the little group of worshipers I worked with would be the dance ministry for our church. When I shared this with the group everyone rejoiced and contributed suggestions for a name. We all decided on the name "Spirit of Worship," abbreviated S.O.W. Our signature Scripture is *John 4:23-24 NIV: "Yet a time is coming and has now come when the true worshipers will worship the Father in the Spirit and in truth, for they are the kind of worshipers the Father seeks. God is spirit, and his worshipers must worship in the Spirit and in truth."*

God opened many doors for S.O.W. to minister and each time the Holy Spirit graced us with His presence. For six months the ministry flourished and then everyone vanished all at once. There were job obligations, health issues, relocation and time restrictions that re-directed the dancers. I was afraid to disappoint my church, but I had no one to be part of the dance ministry. Only a handful of people remained but it wasn't enough to sustain the ministry. To my dismay, the ministry was dissolved 9 months after it began. In the months following, other dance ministers were offered positions in my church to choreograph works. I felt underappreciated but I prayed to see God's perspective and plan in all that was happening. I didn't want to allow anger and bitterness to take root in my heart. I shared my emotional struggle with my husband and he prayed with me. I reached out to the invited ministers to network and the Lord showed me the value of having them come and work in our church. The Lord calls His people in various ways. He called His children to work in His house; thereby, placing them strategically to receive His word. If I treated them indifferently because of my bitterness, they could turn away from the Lord. They needed Christ just as I did and as His ambassador, I needed to represent my Lord well. Bitterness and anger blew away with the wind as God used His winnowing fork to separate me from sin. God gave me compassion for those who entered our church to give themselves to Christ through the arts. I sensed God calling me out of my church to teach and minister to others desiring to receive the skills the Lord allowed me to acquire in my youth.

Over the course of three years, God opened doors for my company. I have been given many opportunities to teach and minister in different churches and schools within the United States and internationally. I would go wherever the Lord would take me to pour out His word. After a season of sitting in my home church, I was offered a position to teach children. I gratefully accepted and it has been my greatest reward to teach our future generation. I don't see them as children but as the leaders of the future. The seeds that we plant in them in their youth will always remain as a part of them. They need to know they are valued and loved. They need to be guided down the right paths and understand their power. Our children need to know how to influence their generation and be bold for Christ. My classes are not just about dance but lessons from Scripture that have life application. I have my students for a short time but when they are with me I pour out what the Holy Spirit gives me.

"Through the praise of children and infants you have established a stronghold against your enemies, to silence the foe and the avenger" (Psalms 8:2 NIV).

My small children participate in class with me and have flourished. My daughter, Denivia choreographed her own dance at the age of seven. She continues to learn and grow as a dance minister, singer and actress. My son, Ayden joins us occasionally and is gifted in dance, song and acting as well. He continues to strive to be the best in activities that he is passionate about. My son, Glenn is a man now. Despite our rocky beginning, God kept him and guided him through life. He is intolerant of injustice and protective by nature. God has used him many times to minister to his peers who are hurting.

I'm truly grateful to God for my three children. They are the arrows in my quiver.

"Children are a heritage from the Lord, offspring a reward from him. Like arrows in the hands of a warrior are children born in one's youth. Blessed is the man whose quiver is full of them. They will not be put to shame when they contend with their opponents in court" (Psalms 127:3-5 NIV).

Chapter 11

~*Purpose for Life*~

In my early years of life, I searched for acceptance and identity. I looked for acceptance in people but was disappointed many times when my search resulted in rejection. I looked for happiness in titles, positions and money but ended up with an empty heart. I believed my identity was the sum of my sins, but that was deception from the enemy of my soul. God restored my passion and transformed my life. Though I had come to a place where my life was better, I knew the Lord would continue to challenge my family to continue to grow.

My plan to become a physical therapist seemed to vanish in a vapor. I thought of other options to make use of my degree and decided to apply to become a teaching fellow. The position would give me summers with my family and help me earn money for expenses. I applied for the position and received an acceptance message in eight weeks. I was very nervous about going forward with the position. I knew it would mean giving up dance again and spending less time with my family as I trained.

In the weeks following my acceptance into the teaching fellows, I was busy meeting deadlines for handing in paperwork and fingerprinting for the Board of education when another offer came for additional training in technology. I accepted the offer and entered the program to train in a school for 5 days.

Everything seemed to be flowing smoothly for me to become a teacher, but there was an uneasy feeling and lack of passion in me to go forward. I thought I would try the onsite training to get experience working in a failing school. I found some of the students difficult to engage and others who were focused. I learned from the training teacher that all of them were returning to high school to try and graduate. I circulated and interviewed students to get feedback on the technology program in the school. The majority of them spoke to me with shyness but were open to my questions. I was told one student I interviewed normally didn't speak in class since experiencing the loss of a sibling. I pondered about the others. What were their stories? Were they looking for an escape like I was? At the end of the week I was sad to go, but I had more insight about teaching in a high needs school. I wanted to help these students but at what cost to my family? I struggled with the decision to stay or leave but decided in the end to give up the position. I felt it would be too much of a strain on my family. With a son about to enter college, a daughter in fourth grade and a son in first grade, there were surely times when I would be needed and not available due to school and work. Now I was back where I started. I didn't have a clear picture of my future. After withdrawing from the teaching fellows I felt like a failure. Would I die without having accomplished anything with my life? I did have a few ministry events planned, so I busied myself executing those plans. It helped keep my mind occupied until I laid in bed at night left with only the thoughts of the days to come. I went on a ministry assignment in Barbados with DMI one month later. The island is beautiful and the people were accommodating. We joined together with the host ministry to be part of two plays. It was beautiful to work in unity with others for a common cause. There were souls that needed to be touched.

My passion for dance was my purpose for service to the Lord. Why couldn't I accept what was so clear? I was anointed to dance and teach. I shared my concerned thoughts with Carlos and as always, my love prayed with me. He has always been the voice of reason, wisdom and love. God connected us divinely and I find it amazing that we can find common ground with such different skillsets. We are able to work together using my creative skills and his logical way of thinking. I'm amazed at how the Lord gives Carlos deep revelation that he, in turn, pours out to our family and his students. He inspires me to move forward in the assignments the Lord gave to us. We have our individual focus on purpose, but the Lord revealed the greater connected purpose for us as one flesh. There is power in unity and greater clarity when we seek God together. We share a Kingdom purpose to be lifelong learners and to move forward to disciple the nations.

"Therefore go and make disciples of all nations, baptizing them in the name of the Father and of the Son and of the Holy Spirit, (v. 20) and teaching them to obey everything I have commanded you. And surely I am with you always, to the very end of the age" (Matthew 28:19-20 NIV).

A Threefold Cord

And if one prevail against him,
two shall withstand him;
and a threefold cord is not quickly broken.
Ecclesiastes 4:12 (KJV)

Chapter 12

~Healing Old Wounds~

We all experience offense at the hands of other people in our lives. The more you care for someone, the greater the offense you suffer. I held on to offenses that eventually turned my heart to stone. God restored my heart to flesh and through His word revealed to me that I needed to forgive and ask for forgiveness. I suffered silently for decades holding the memories of hurt in my past, but God didn't want me to remain in that place. I repented to the Lord and asked Him to help me forgive all those who offended me. I have come to a place in my life that I have forgiven my ex-husband and asked him to forgive me as well. He has a relationship with our son, Glenn and has since remarried and lives a better life. My mother no longer has a relationship with Chris and I have forgiven him for the hurt he caused our family. God continues to mend relationships and heal old wounds that were allowed to fester for too long.

> "For if you forgive other people when they sin against you, your heavenly Father will also forgive you. But if you do not forgive others their sins, your Father will not forgive your sins" (Matthew 6:14-15 NIV).

~Daddy~

My father has remained a tug in my heart. Even today I find that I have a strong sensitivity to the need for my father's affection. I have seen countless men, women and children share stories of the hurt they experienced due to the absence of their father. Each time I hear a story my heart aches and tears flow freely as I relate to a life without a father. I'm grateful that my father is still alive and that I can hear his voice and hug him when I need to. For my entire life my father has been accessible whenever I've needed him. I don't always get the response I expect but at least I have him. My father is older now and physically unable to live in cold harsh weather. He prepared for several years to move to Florida. I wasn't prepared for my reaction when he told me he was finally leaving. He was traveling to Florida 4 times a year to stay a month at a time looking for a house. He had finally found a house and closed the deal. I called him for his 61st birthday—a day late, as I recall—as I returned home after walking my children to school. The news uprooted something I didn't know was buried inside of me. Suddenly I was 10 years old again, watching my father depart from our family. He would no longer be a short commute from me but hundreds of miles away. I wouldn't see him as often as I used to and would be limited to yearly visits. My daddy was leaving again. I felt my eyes fill with warm tears, but I hid my emotion from him as we spoke. I wiped my tears and continued our conversation as if nothing was wrong. When I was alone I did cry. I let every buried emotion flood out as I allowed myself to love my father. No matter what happened in the past he was still my father and I wanted him to be close. I sat for a long time remembering all of the good times we had together. I didn't want him to feel guilty about moving, I just wanted him to know that I loved him and would miss him. I realized then that I'd forgiven my father for leaving us years ago. The anger and bitterness that once occupied my spirit was no longer present. I sat and spoke with my father to tell him that I loved him and he was always in my heart. He cried and told me he was proud of me and felt comforted that I'd married a good man who would take care of our children and me. I thanked my heavenly Father for never leaving me and bringing healing and deliverance for all I held in my heart. I'm grateful for "a Father's love."

"See what great love the Father has lavished on us, that we should be called children of God! And that is what we are! The reason the world does not know us is that it did not know him" (1 John 3:1 NIV).

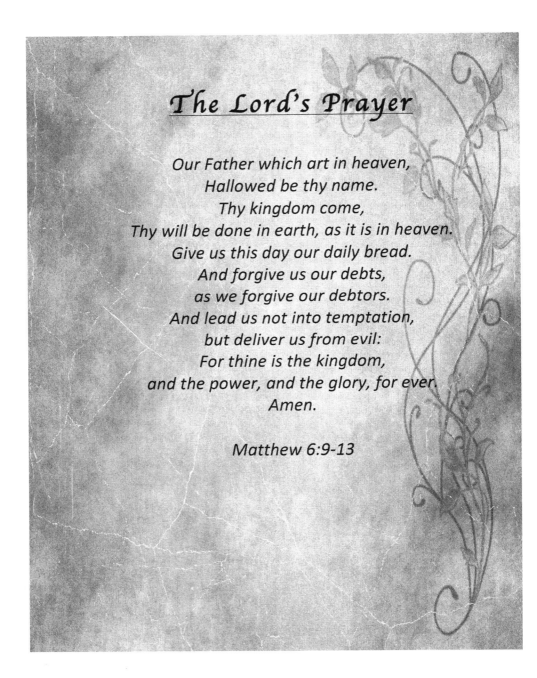

The Lord's Prayer

Our Father which art in heaven,
Hallowed be thy name.
Thy kingdom come,
Thy will be done in earth, as it is in heaven.
Give us this day our daily bread.
And forgive us our debts,
as we forgive our debtors.
And lead us not into temptation,
but deliver us from evil:
For thine is the kingdom,
and the power, and the glory, for ever.
Amen.

Matthew 6:9-13

~Epilogue~

I pray this book blesses someone who struggles with abuse and low self-esteem.

I struggled with my identity most of my life and searched for acceptance in all the wrong places. I found my identity in Jesus Christ who restored my passion and anointed the gifts He created in me. I learned to conform to Jesus and look for His purpose in all things instead of my own purpose. My purpose for dancing was to gain acceptance for myself. The Lord's purpose is to gain lives for His kingdom.

There is power in movement. When we dance, people are moved by God's message through us. There is an activation of faith within them so healing and deliverance can take place. We are transformed from glory to glory in increasing measure as we worship our Lord in the dance.

I know now that all the dance experience I have had will be used to bless others to be dance ministers for the Lord. I will pour out all that God has given me to take back the art of dance for His Kingdom.

When I reflect on all my life experiences, I can appreciate the hardships and the good times. I can see God's hand in shaping my life. I could never have imagined anything good could come from adversity, but the Lord transformed my heart so I could see things differently. I was a lost soul looking for my purpose, but I needed to learn to seek God for answers. There were times I thought I was alone and God didn't hear my prayers but He never left me. God was present throughout my life, protecting me from death, preserving me from becoming weary and giving me a way out of misery. He gave me favor with so many people to get the best education and training for what I was purposed to do.

When I finally decided to repent and live for Christ, prayers that I had long forgotten were answered. I realize now how undeserving I am of all He has done for me. I listened to so many people in church shout and sing about the blood of Jesus and never knew the significance. How could blood wash anything?

There is life in the blood. The New International Version of Leviticus 17:11 states, *"For the life of a creature is in the blood, and I have given it to you to make atonement for yourselves on the altar; it is the blood that makes atonement for one's life."* Blood atones for our sins. Animals were slaughtered as a sin offering before the Lamb of God, Jesus. Jesus paid for all our transgressions when His blood was shed in the crucifixion. I can never repay what was done for me. Jesus gave all He could give for me.

Psalm 49:8, NIV declares, "the ransom for a life is costly, no payment is ever enough—"

Writing my testimony has been difficult. I have gone through many emotional episodes to simply recall and express my journey in the best way I remember. I'm grateful that God has taken me on this course of life, through the good and bad, because I know it led to Him. I have been able to overcome hard times with God preparing the way before me. I have been able to survive death because of Jesus' intercession. I have seen many in my family come to Christ as God promised. God answers prayer. He loves us and I am a living witness. My testimony serves as a message of hope to those who will receive. Above all, search the Scriptures for truth and God will take you through your suffering.

If you have a testimony, I want to encourage you to share it; write it down. It will serve as a message of hope to others, even those beyond your years.

"So do not be ashamed of the testimony about our Lord or of me his prisoner. Rather, join with me in suffering for the gospel, by the power of God" (2 Timothy 1:8 NIV).
"And they overcame him by the blood of the Lamb and by the word of their testimony: and they loved not their lives unto the death" (Revelation 12:11 KJV).

Appendix A

~*Salvation for All*~

Grace is the free gift that offers salvation to all people. We have all sinned against God. It doesn't matter where you come from or what you've done, God gives grace to you freely. If you committed a crime there are consequences according to the law. You would be arrested and informed of the charges against you and sent to trial. In the court, there is a prosecutor, lawyer and judge. The lawyer is there to defend you, the prosecutor is there to present a case against you, and the judge is there to pronounce a specific penalty for your crime. In the same way there are consequences for our immoral acts against God. Our lawyer is Jesus, Satan is the prosecutor, and God is our judge. God's word says the penalty of sin is death but God sent Jesus to save us. Jesus accepted our death sentence even though we are guilty of the accusations against us. He died so that we could live. The price Jesus paid is enough for everyone because of His innocence.

Why did Jesus die for us?

Jesus gave His life for us because He loves us. In the same way a father or mother would give their life for their child.

You are eligible to become a child of God regardless of your past offenses, current lifestyle, background, or family history. Jesus is waiting for you to acknowledge Him so that you can be brought back to God. To be reconciled to God you must commit to turning away from sin and dedicate your life to Jesus Christ. When you do this you will become a child of God. You will be free from bondage with a new hope in Jesus Christ.

"If you declare with your mouth, "Jesus is Lord," and believe in your heart that God raised him from the dead, you will be saved. For it is with your heart that you believe and are justified, and it is with your mouth that you profess your faith and are saved." Romans 10:9-10 (NIV)

If you believe Jesus died for your sins and you are ready to dedicate your life to Him, then declare with your all of your heart the prayer below out loud.

Father in heaven, I come to you in the name of Jesus to acknowledge to you that I am a sinner and ask for your forgiveness. Father I ask you to cleanse me of unrighteousness. I choose to turn away from sin.

I believe you sent your only begotten son Jesus, born of the Virgin Mary to die for my sins on Calvary. I believe He resurrected from the dead on the third day and is seated at your right hand.
Lord your Word says if we declare with our mouth that Jesus is Lord, and believe in our heart that you raised Him from the dead, we will be saved. Father right now I declare Jesus is Lord of my life. Jesus, I ask you to come into my life and I surrender to your Lordship. On this day, I give up a life that is unpleasing in your sight. From this day forward I live for you Lord.

Thank you for saving me and for your grace.
In Jesus Name
Amen.

_____(Name)
accepted   Jesus   as   Lord   and   Savior   on
_____ *(date)*

" *For the grace of God has appeared that offers salvation to all people. It teaches us to say "No" to ungodliness and worldly passions, and to live self-controlled, upright and godly lives in this present age, while we wait for the blessed hope—the appearing of the glory of our great God and Savior, Jesus Christ, who gave himself for us to redeem us from all wickedness and to purify for himself a people that are his very own, eager to do what is good."*
Titus 2:11-14 (NIV)

"Yet to all who did receive him, to those who believed in his name, he gave the right to become children of God."
John 1:12 (NIV)

Congratulations!
If you've made this commitment you are a child of God. Your next step is to join a church in your area. Allow God to connect your passion with purpose.

Appendix B

~Present Suffering Future Glory~

A message is for those who are hurting

We all experience suffering in our lives. None are exempt from trials and tribulations.

Whether you are dealing with abuse, rejection, failed relationships, offenses, or discouragement, faith in Christ gives hope. There may be times when you feel like God has forgotten you but He hasn't. The Bible says, "He is close to the broken hearted and saves the crushed in spirit." (Psalm 34:18). Take a moment to reflect on your life and see how the Lord was present during difficult times. Even in the times you couldn't pray through your brokenness God's Spirit helped you by praying for you. (Romans 8:26-27).

God's word will give you guidance, strength and peace. God will restore you.

"And the God of all grace, who called you to his eternal glory in Christ, after you have suffered a little while, will himself restore you and make you strong, firm and steadfast." 1 Peter 5:10 (NIV)

When you face trials and tribulations you learn to persevere. Your character will change with every situation you face. After you have made it through a trial, you can look to the future with hope.

"Consider it pure joy, my brothers and sisters, whenever you face trials of many kinds, because you know that the testing of your faith produces perseverance. Let

95

perseverance finish its work so that you may be mature and complete, not lacking anything." James 1:2-4 (NIV)

"Therefore, since we have been justified through faith, we have peace with God through our Lord Jesus Christ, through whom we have gained access by faith into this grace in which we now stand. And we boast in the hope of the glory of God. Not only so, but we also glory in our sufferings, because we know that suffering produces perseverance; perseverance, character; and character, hope. And hope does not put us to shame, because God's love has been poured out into our hearts through the Holy Spirit, who has been given to us." Romans 5: 1-5 (NIV)

" I consider that our present sufferings are not worth comparing with the glory that will be revealed in us." Romans 8:18 (NIV)

For those who are living with abuse

Abuse is cruel or violent treatment of a person that can be verbal, physical, psychological, sexual abuse or neglect. Victims of abuse can range from infants to elderly, in every race, religion and social class. Abuse can happen to anyone.

You must acknowledge you are in an abusive relationship. You can do this by evaluating your own feelings.

Are you afraid to make your suspected abuser angry? Do you avoid speaking or feel fearful this person will explode. Do you feel helpless and numb? Do you think you deserve to be abused? If you answered yes to any of the questions you may be a victim of abuse. It is not acceptable for you to be abused. You deserve freedom from maltreatment. Seek help to free yourself. Tell someone that you are being abused. There is no shame in what happened to you. You are the victim. If you are living with your abuser, seek a separate living arrangement to remove yourself from danger. God would never harm you nor should anyone else.

"For I know the plans I have for you," declares the Lord, "plans to prosper you and not to harm you, plans to give you hope and a future." Jeremiah 29:11 (NIV)

The National Domestic Violence Hotline
 1-800-799-7233
www.thehotline.org

 National Network to End Domestic Violence
www.nnedv.org

~Bibliography~

Hayden, Lynn M. *Dance in the Church What's the Pointe?* Eustis Florida, SPS Publications, 2000. Print.

Silberling, Murray. *Dancing for Joy, A Biblical Approach to Praise and Worship*. Baltimore Maryland, Lederer Books, 1995. Print.

Clark, Heather. *Dance as the Spirit Moves, A Practical guide to Worship Dance*. Shippensburg PA, Destiny Image Publishers Inc. 2009. Print.

Stevenson, Ann. *Dance! God's Holy Purpose.* Shippensburg PA, Destiny Image Publishers Inc. 1998. Print.

~About the Author~

Alicia Rivera is the founder and artistic director of *Jubilee Dance Studio Inc.,* Assistant Artistic Director of *Ruach Dance Company* and Curriculum Planner of *The Worship Academy*. Alicia has 34 years of dance experience that includes training in Classical Ballet, Modern, Jazz, Afro Caribbean, and West African dance. She also has over 20 years experience as a dance instructor and choreographer. She has worked with both children and adults of all ages and levels in various schools, YMCA and churches.

Alicia majored in dance liberal arts/dance at *Borough of Manhattan Community College* where she started a dance club. She served as president of the dance club for 2 years. Her duties included, organizing rehearsals and performances for the school, choreographing dance works for various school events.

In the early 1990's, Alicia worked professionally with dance companies such as, *Forces of Nature, Alpha Omega, Rod Rogers,* and *Joan Miller Dance Players.* During her time with these companies she also worked with individual choreographers *Lenny Williams, Fred Benjamin, Frank Hatchett, Eleo Pomare,* and *Chuck*

Davis. Some of the works she performed include *"Ancestral Earths"*, *"Blue Soweto"*, *"Baharini"*, *"Tabernacle"*, and *"Essence"*.

In 2010, Alicia graduated with a Bachelor of Science degree in biology from *College of Mount Saint Vincent.* Shortly after completing college, God called her to dance for Him. In 2011-2014, Alicia ministered in the production *"Nativity"* with *Dance Ministry Institute.* Since then she has remained a minister with *Dance Ministry Institute* and has also ministered in a variety of settings with her company under *Jubilee Dance Studio.* She has hosted two Dancing *for Him* conferences and facilitates multiple workshops in various states. Alicia has served as a dance minister and instructor/choreographer for international missions companies, *Adventures in Missions, Dance Dimensions,* and *Praise Academy of Dance.*

Alicia is a licensed teacher and ordained dance minister with *Dancing for Him Ministries.* She is also a certified teacher and representative with *Living Dance International.* Alicia currently serves as a dance artist/instructor at her home church. She has also served as a Sunday school teacher and dance leader for *Spirit of Worship Dance Ministry.* Alicia serves on the *Nehemiah Council* for *Break Free Dance Studio.* She is on the Board of Directors for *Year of Jubilee Corp.* and Administrator of *Leviticus 25 Financial Ministries.* She and her husband Carlos Rivera reside in New York with their three children.

Threshing Floor
African Movement Workshop DVD

Subjects include:
Preparing the land
Sowing seed
Separating wheat and tares
Harvesting
Threshing tools/ methods
Celebration

Threshing Worship is a time of threshing when God separates the chaff in our lives. When we enter into worship we step onto God's threshing floor where he deals with those things, which need to be removed from our lives.

"I baptize you with water for repentance. But after me comes one who is more powerful than I, whose sandals I am not worthy to carry. He will baptize you with the Holy Spirit and fire. His winnowing fork is in his hand, and he will clear his threshing floor, gathering his wheat into the barn and burning up the chaff with unquenchable fire." Matthew 3:11-12 (NIV)

**To order DVD or host a workshop near you go to
www.jubileedance.org**

Visit Online:
Website: **www.jubileedance.org**
Facebook: **www.facebook.com/Jubileedancestudio**
Pinterest: **www.pinterest.com/jubileedanceorg/**
Twitter: **www.twitter.com/jubileedanceorg**
Linkedin: **www.linkedin.com/in/AliciaRiveraJubileeDance**
Youtube: **www.youtube.com/c/AliciaRiveraJubileeDance**
Google+: **www.google.com/+AliciaRiveraJubileeDance**